UnBrokable*
II

The 2nd 10 Reasons Why People Go Broke Despite Working

Brad Kong

Disclaimer

This is the **2nd Edition** of *UnBrokable* II* from UnBrokable* series; these are the full title and subtitle of this book:

UnBrokable* II:
*The 2nd 10 Reasons Why People Go **Broke** Despite Working*

   I wrote *only* "***The 2nd 10 Reasons Why Broke***" on the front cover *intentionally* for rhyme, simplicity and focus.

   The graphic on this book cover is from Edit.org. I use the site to design my covers; it provides book cover templates with its copy-righted images to writers who paid "annual memberships."

   I do have three proofs of my membership to Edit.org, payment receipt for the membership through Paypal and reference address to the image of the site. I am writing this because I received emails regarding my "book cover images" twice; both of which were resolved within a day. I decided to stick to my own or edit.org's images since I cannot keep getting copyright emails. If you have any issue regarding my cover art, feel free to contact me: I will be more than happy to provide the three proofs again.

Also by Brad Kong

UnBrokable* series:

Introduction to UnBrokable*
UnBrokable* I (Chapter 1 to 10)

UnBrokable* Sketch series:

Introduction to UnBrokable* (Chapter 1 to 5)
Intro to UnBrokable* Large Print

UnBrokable* I (Chapter 1 to 10)
UnBrokable* II (Chapter 11 to 20)
UnBrokable* III (Chapter 21 to 30)
UnBrokable* IV (Chapter 31 to 40)
UnBrokable* V (Chapter 41 to 50)
UnBrokable* VI (Chapter 51 to 60)
UnBrokable* VII (Chapter 61 to 70)
UnBrokable* VIII (Chapter 71 to 80)

UnBrokable* (Chapter 1 to 80)

Brad Short Story Collection I:

Robbery at Cyb Knight
How to Get Rid of Ladies
11 Girls I had Loved
Say No To TSLA
3 Ways to Avoid Divorce
15 Ways to Keep Your Teeth Healthy
5 Moments When I Felt Sorry For My Cat

Corn Dog Grandpas
Condo Chronicle
How to Lose 40 Pounds

Brad Short Story Collection II:

15 Things You Didn't Know About Korea
3 Reasons Why We Need to Buy a Home Early
Why Are CDs Super Important?
Say No To TSLA (2nd Edition)
Large Pizza for $5
30 Reasons Why I am Great

Praise for *UnBrokable*

"This is the best book I have ever read. I am saying this only because Brad is my husband."

-Tsina D,

A housewife and teacher

"I cannot believe my dad wrote this much thick book. He must be a genius."

-Yuna K,

An elementary school student

"I am proud of my son who wrote a book in English."

-Mrs. Jin,

A wealthy woman

"Publishing this book is a celebration itself. Write your name on the next page if you bought this for a gift."

-Brad K,

A philosopher, writer, publisher, book designer and investor

UnBrokable*

Dear _____

This book is my gift for you.

It has been helpful for me, so I hope it will be helpful for you as well.

Thank you always.

Sincerely,

From _____

For All the Honest Workers

Struggling Everyday

Foreword

So many books out there from Self-Help and Financial Gurus talk about personal finances in abstract terms. These are folks who make millions selling books telling us what to do. Here is something new and refreshing, however. The author relates his real-life experiences in personal finance. Not only is there a lot of good advice in here, it is an interesting look into someone else's life.

It seems we are at a time in history where everyone is struggling to get ahead. But then again, if we look back in history, it has always been this way. The inflation of today pales to that of the 1970's. The unemployment of a few years ago was nothing like that era, either. What is frustrating for so many is that even "making good money" people are living "paycheck to paycheck" and wondering where the money all went. I know I fell into this trap!

The author illustrates how people go broke even while making a hefty salary, and provides a guide to being "UnBrokable" - a term he has coined. And apparently it works - he retired at 40, not from selling self-help books (like so many Gurus do) but by being careful with money.

There is a lot here to learn from. And it's only just getting started!

Robert P. Bell

Georgia

USA

Mr. Robert P. Bell is a retired Patent Attorney, self-made millionaire and founder of the popular blog named Living stingy (http://livingstingy.blogspot.com). He has written in the last 15 years since 2008 and helped tons of people get out of debts and money problems. He is well known for his humorous but sharp writing style and has influenced myriads of writers and bloggers including Brad Kong.

Contents

UnBrokable* II

UnBrokable* III

UnBrokable* IV

UnBrokable* V

UnBrokable* VI

UnBrokable* VII

UnBrokable VIII

Prologue

Dying poor is a shame especially in wealthy countries.
It is not all about money; it shows how we have lived.
-Brad Kong

This is me sitting on the Ferrari in Miami, FL in 2003. Then, I didn't
expect I would go abysmally broke and suffer for a long time. I had to
work as a weekend dishwasher for 7 years from 2015.

Jack Whittaker was a construction businessman in
Putnam County, WV; he was known as the winner of a
lottery jackpot of $315 million[1] in the Powerball in 2002.
He was a millionaire already with a net worth of $17 M
even before winning – a rich man won a huge lottery.

---

[1] USD

Oddly, a series of unfortunate events started happening to him afterward. First, a guy named Tribble, the boyfriend of Whittaker's granddaughter Brandi, was found dead from drug overdose in Whittaker's home in September, 2004; three months later, Brandi herself was also found dead at the age of 17; it shows that cocaine and methadone were found in her body. Five years later, Ginger, who was the mother of Brandi and Whittaker's daughter, was also found dead at age 42 in Daniels, WV; the police suspected it could be the OD again. Then, Whittaker's home in Bland County, VA, was reported to be on fire in 2016. Finally, Whittaker himself passed away following a long illness at the age of 72 in 2020: *Why did the luckiest guy in the world pass away early after losing all his children?*

Han Liu[2] was a Chinese billionaire, the former chairman of Hanlong Group, which is known for mining businesses in China. His assets were officially claimed at $6 billion by the time he passed away at the age of 49 in 2015. He was convicted of murdering 8 people and running a mafia gang for his businesses; he was executed by the law enforcement in China. His last words had been viral online: "Life is short; *we don't have to live too diligently for more money.* I will have a small store next life and live happily with my family."

---

[2] Liu was his last name: Wrong order in Wikipedia.

I agree with the lessons above: I don't have to work to death, make a lot, spend more, leave a fortune to others and die; I do not want to *grind* myself to donate more. In the book *Psychology of money* by Housel, there is a story of a man named Read; he was a janitor for 42 years, made a fortune out of the stock market, left $8 million to a hospital and passed away. I know a similar case of Groner who worked as a secretary for 43 years, made profit out of the Abbott shares, left $7 million to a local college and died. They were undoubtedly honorable. But, seriously, *what's the point?* What would be the thing they regretted the most? As long as I have enough, **I conclude that the best reward I can give to myself is *working less*.** I may not need a luxury car, but I like to save myself from being offended by bosses and customers.

Have you ever been a dishwasher before? **If you don't fully agree with this book, you might not have been broke enough.** I believe that a guaranteed way to stay *insufferable* is staying away from the reasons causing poverty. Coincidentally, I was in Chinatown Chicago the other day; it had some Korean shops, which I found were crowded. It took forever for South Korea to be wealthy. Ironically, once we[3] become rich, I learned that we can make money out of it: *Being rich itself can be a new source of income.*

---

[3] Not Koreans, but all of us who read this book

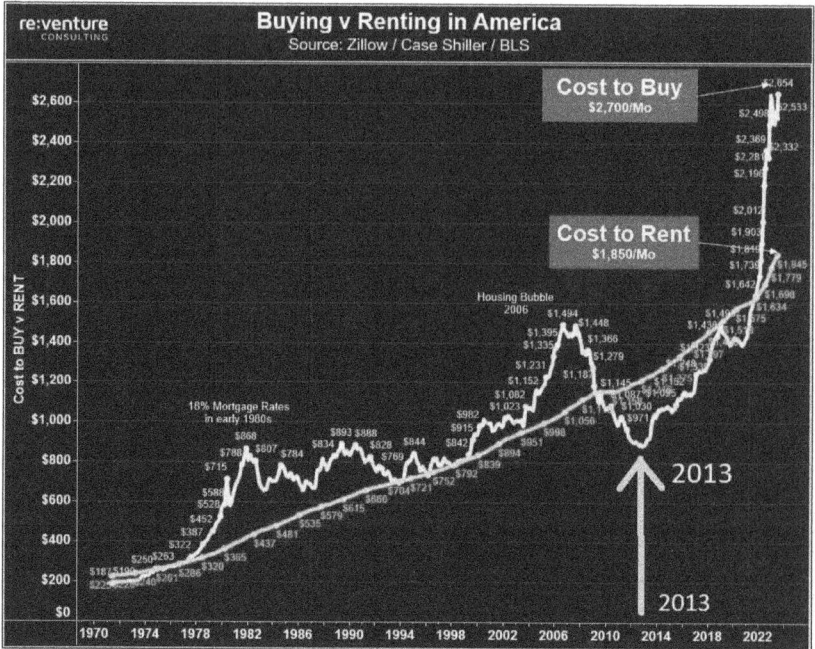

re:venture CONSULTING

Buying v Renting in America
Source: Zillow / Case Shiller / BLS

Cost to Buy $2,700/Mo

Cost to Rent $1,850/Mo

Housing Bubble 2006

18% Mortgage Rates in early 1980s

2013

2013

I bought my home in November, 2013. I didn't know it was the lowest price ever in the 21st century (source from Zillow).

My net worth has increased 8 times in the past decade. I had $80,000 CDs and some cash in the bank in 2013: How do I remember it? I bought my condo at full price of $60,000[4] that year; my real estate agent asked me to submit proof of funds in advance; I didn't know what to do, so I got a receipt from the ATM and gave it to her. Now I have over a $650,000 portfolio, not including my residence, as of 2023. This growth has probably resulted from inheritance, investment success, salaries and frugality. But I would say that "not having rent or mortgages" played the most crucial role.

---

[4] It was low due to depression as it's up to $175,000 in 2023.

I enjoyed my life; until I couldn't. And some of us may not since a recession may approach in 2024. Maybe this book is not for the super-rich; probably not even for the middle-class or mildly poor. I had been in a desperate situation myself, especially around 2009. My business wasn't doing well; the subprime mortgage crisis broke out; my car was a decade old; those horrible mechanics kept overcharging me amid despair; then my daughter was born in 2010. I couldn't waste even a single cent for years, but I was able to manage to buy a small condo thanks to my parents; the only advantage was that all the house prices collapsed significantly due to foreclosures by the heavy depression. This book is not about making more, but rather suffering less for those: **Unlucky people who have no idea how to get out of poverty.**

The Ferrari photo above was taken 20 years ago in 2003; back then, I had no idea how much trouble I was about to go through; I was stupid in my late 20s. Now I know that being wealthy is a combination of small skills, knowledge and *luck*. On the contrary, being broke can happen easily on no significant grounds.

* * *

Charles Bukowski (1920 – 1994) was an American poet considered "the laureate of low-life" in the 1970s; he bought his first house 23 years *later* than me. His net worth was over $4 million by the time he passed away:

How did that happen? Mr. Bukowski was often considered a drunk loser, but I found out that he and I share a few things in common. First of all, we both started writing careers after our 40s; both had or have one daughter. We both had worked for low income physical jobs for a while; we both inherited some money from parents after becoming middle aged men. Also we both were born in foreign countries, originally.

But it shows that he bought his first house with a mortgage at the age of 58 in 1979; I bought my condo with cash at the age of 40 in 2013. Then, it took an extra 5 years for him to pay off his mortgage (which was fast). As a result, he ended up buying his house 23 years slower than me: What made him delay this long?

It is natural if someone goes broke when he or she does not have a job. But some live poor forever even though they work full-time. **More ironically, some live wealthy for good without having a job**: *How?* For instance, my mother was initially from a poor family (typical among old Koreans) and never had a job for decades. But she has been in the top wealthy class in the country for most of her adult life: What happened?

* * *

Again, let me start this 2nd edition of *UnBrokable* *II* by congratulating you: Picking up this book means that you are, at least, one step closer to wealth. This series will be a practical, unorthodox or alternative guide to stay away from *brokeness*; we will talk about unique reasons, examples and facts; it is my memoir, too. ***"Brokeness" (not brokenness[5]) is a noun meaning "the characteristic of not having enough money."***

Have you ever been broke before even though you have a job? Have you been short of money despite working full-time? People may not get broke automatically, especially in wealthy countries; if some are poor despite the fact that they work to death, I think there must be reasons. *What do you believe makes a person poor?* **Why do some still rent an apartment after working 12 hours a day for 30 years?** I had witnessed a couple of those closely for 7 years.

"UnBrokable*" may not be a word we can find in a dictionary yet as I coined it: **A person who cannot be financially broke is "UnBrokable."** The opposite of *Les Miserable.* I think that there is a big misconception in our lives: If we work hard, we will be rich. Nothing can be further from the truth; *in fact, I suspect that working longer can make us poorer.* Some live painfully by exploiting themselves; "working longer" is one way.

This book is a collection of my own survival stories in a sense; I am a middle-aged man with a wife and a daughter from the Midwest. I think my American life can be divided into four periods since 1999.

---

[5] *Broke**nn**ess* means "a condition in which something is badly damaged."

1. Colleges: Cornell and SUNY at Buffalo (1999-2005)
2. Business: Cyb Knight Video Games (2006-2014)
3. Employment: A nursing home (2015-2022)
4. Investor and writer (2022 - current)

Or I can divide the 24 years by jobs:

- College banquet (2001 - 2002)
- eBay and Amazon seller (2003 - 2015)
- Cyb Knight Games Owner (2006-2014)
- Nursing home dishwasher (2015-2022)
- Investor and writer (2011-current)

There are other jobs with licenses I prefer not to go in depth now (pharmacy technician and medical coder). Also I have worked for myriads of small jobs since high school in Korea: convenience store clerk, bar kitchen helper, military soldier, etc.

* * *

Out of all those jobs, the recent *weekend dishwasher* gave me the strongest inspiration to write *UnBrokable** series. The nursing home I worked at is within walking distance from my home. I had a chance to volunteer to work there one day in 2015; unexpectedly, that brought me a permanent weekend position. Then, I had not done anything for a year after closing out my video game store permanently in 2014. At the end of the work, they suddenly wondered (literally begged) if I could do the job at least every weekend. Now I see the reason why as I asked similar questions to other volunteers or temp workers myself. For some reason, those nursing homes always need employees while no one is excited to work there. Since they suggested a reasonable pay and plenty of food from the kitchens, I accepted that offer. I had the job only on weekends for six years and on Sunday for a year, which means totally close to seven years.

I never liked that job much since it was physically hard, but have to admit that it has been helpful for my life in some ways. First, I had chances to meet a lot of people I would have not without it; there are types of people doing dishwashing for life. No offense, but **I think I was able to see some mandatory reasons they all had in common: The reasons why they never get out of poverty.** I think I had good chances to take a look at their lives; some were *truly great* guys. Secondly, the job had brought me physical strength; I have lost a lot of weight, especially in the beginning and gained muscles continuously throughout the years. Thirdly, these weekend extra salaries, bonus and free food still helped me build up my savings faster.

There could be millions of reasons why people go broke: gambling, drug addictions, car accidents, etc; we cannot help those getting into obvious troubles. **Nonetheless, there are millions of people apparently not doing anything wrong, but always being broke while**

working; many have nothing left in their bank accounts after some payments are withdrawn at the end of every month.

* * *

Do you know when I had the hardest time with money? While I worked at the video game store, my daughter was born in 2010. When a baby is born, parents need more money while physically exhausted to take care of the baby. Incidentally, the mortgage bubble burst in 2008 and I remember that severe depression came from 2009: The subprime mortgage crisis. I guess that businesses must have a hard time these days as COVID pandemic has been from 2020; the impact may not be over quickly. While I had wasted a massive amount of my parents' money only to keep my business open, the only good thing I did was buy a condo in full. Since the economy collapsed in 2008, there had been plenty of foreclosures, short sales and discounted houses on the market. Getting rid of my rent for good was the only upside during that era.

After having difficulty with money myself and watching people struggling, I started wondering what really makes a laborer in trouble: **Is there any practical trap to make full-timers broke even in wealthy countries?** While working in the nursing home, I saw dishwashers still renting apartments even after *30* years of employment. They occasionally worked *double*, which means working up to 15 hours a day: **Where did all their money go?**

Are you ready to jump into 80 chapters with thousands of examples? **All the episodes are either from my personal experience or true events throughout history.** I hope this will be the longest series you've ever finished since you cannot put it down. By the time we reach the epilogue, I anticipate that we can be more mature, knowledgeable and a bit closer to wealth.

11

Not Going Against Destiny

If we stay with poverty too long, it will never get off.
-Brad Kong

There is a movie titled *The Hurt Locker* starring Renner. The main actor is an American soldier in Iraq and his specialty is disassembling bombs: the leader of the Explosive Ordnance Disposal (EOD) unit. He survived many dangerous missions and returned home safely in the end. However, he was bored with routine civilian life and started another hellish mission again.

Believe it or not, I think a lot of people live like him. Some get back to bad relationships, horrible jobs or financial despair again until their lives are over. How can we get out of vicious downward spirals? How can we be different from a hamster running in a spinner? **My recommendation is to have a habit to try something new whenever possible**; a mindset of *"Try everything at least once"* can help us get out of current repetitions. I guess we can start it by trying a new restaurant or menu. Maybe we can read a book we would never imagine reading before.

Do you know why a majority of lottery winners go bankrupt several years after winning? I think they failed to challenge their destinies; they didn't resist against their predestined poverty. If we live in destitution for more than a decade, it can become our fate; some people feel comfortable being indigent. Some ticket winners probably would have felt uncomfortable getting a lot of money all at once; they spent it quickly or even gave it away to others until they felt comfortable as before.

I think the other way around is also possible, though. There are people comfortable sitting on money. Actually, some probably cannot put up with not having enough. I have made about $35,000 capital gain out of the stock market by August 2023; I had about 70 company stocks and 40 company bonds, then. One day, Diebold filed for bankruptcy and one of my bonds was wiped out as a result; they returned only $100 after my $1,500 was gone.

You know what the issue was, though? **I couldn't put up with owning only 39 company bonds.** For no reason, it bothered me like hell, so I bought a McDonald's bond to make 40 bond companies in my portfolio; I felt relieved, finally. These types of people can be broke temporarily, but always come back to be sufficient financially. They just hate the feeling when they don't have what they used to have. Maybe they have been wealthy for long, so affluence have become their destinies.

* * *

There was a girl server named Vanessa when I worked at the smaller restaurant in the nursing home in 2015; I believe she was about 20 year-old Latin American; I saw that her divorced parents were originally from El Salvador on her Facebook; her mother had four children from a couple of relationships and she was the second child; she has one older brother and two younger brothers. I do not remember her good at serving; she made a lot of hustle and bustle unnecessarily in the kitchen (to get attention from boys I assume). Whenever she brought a large amount of dirty dishes on a tray to the dishwashers, she often slammed them on the counter, which was rude by itself, then a few broke occasionally. I did not like the female manager from Jordan who was a close friend to her as well; both made my life uncomfortable, then.

She ended up quitting the job in 2016 and I found out that she was pregnant already and had one son at the age of 21 on her Facebook later; it seems that was the reason why she quit although her family was struggling. The father of her baby was a Mexican boy waiter working together in the restaurant. I thought this is too early to start a family since all these two had were just a couple of high school diplomas. **More importantly, in my opinion, 21 was too early for a man to get into a "prison" called marriage.** I am not blindly against marriage, but I guess it is true that prison and marriage share some points in common (both may provide stable lives, too). By 2016, both of this couple did not have a college education, job or income, but ended up having a baby: Who does not know how to make a baby? Personally, I don't necessarily consider having a baby early as an accomplishment. It was not extremely hard for me, at least.

I saw her photos only with her son without the waiter boy on her Facebook when I checked it last time in 2021. I guess it's possible they might have gotten separated already. **It's true that it was too much to ask for a 21 years-old boy to stick to only one woman for the rest of his life.** I know this is what a modern marriage requires, but is it honestly allowable to you in a sense of nature? If so, do we have to start it as early as possible? Alternatively, I think a man can marry a little later in his life after he learns that there is nothing much special about other women. I don't think shackling a young boy by social rules works out well all the time.

As a result, it seems to me that she followed the destiny of her divorced mother exactly. Only difference is her mother has four, but she has one for now; both seem to be alcoholic, too, according to their photos on Facebook. Statistically, Latin Americans tend to have more babies at younger ages in America. I cannot blame all the Mexican descendants since some never get married. Here is one important question, though: Could she have gone against her destiny? Could she have gone against the general trend of Latinas? Could she have tried to be a little different from her mother? I also noticed that every single one of her friends was Mexicans on Facebook. Maybe she could not see beyond her Hispanic world. Is this what's happening to me or all of us by chance?

I have a father who has made an incredible amount of wealth out of nothing in Korea. That is great, but he also has unnecessarily showing off and feisty characters. **Am I going against my predestination[6]?** I think I do not spend money to show off like him, at least, as I do not even own a car. Still, do I inherit his bad characteristics, instead of his business skills? He got divorced, but am I a good husband or parent to my own family? I think I should be selectively aggressive from now on. I have never liked my father since he had been angry all the time. Still, I cannot be generous to everyone since there are obvious assholes. I think it's important for me to be awake as often as possible and act reasonably based on situations.

* * *

Some people reject happiness or even money by habits. Some women reject a great guy because he looks too good to be true; they have hypnotized themselves that it cannot be real since nothing *great* has happened to them; probably, that has been a fact. However, often, some just do not try anything new; for example, a few have never been out of their home States. I am not saying that we ought to take risks: **I am suggesting that we should**

---

[6] Already defined destiny

not go back to our original bad destinies only because we are so comfortable with them.

Believe it or not, I think some people choose misfortune voluntarily: The common point is that they are familiar with misfortune; the most common could be a lot of them have grown up with unfortunate childhoods. **Some choose familiar bad lives rather than happy unfamiliar ones.** Whenever a good thing happens, some think they do not deserve it, subconsciously. I used to be one of those, too; I kept the weekend dishwashing job far too long, even after I got wealthy; it took quite a while to let go of the drudgery and admit I don't have to do that. I was uncomfortable living only on dividends, even after I have done that for a decade.

It is possible that we may live unhappily now for nothing. Therefore, it is crucial for us to have a habit to try something new unless it is dangerous: I think it is an efficient way to *break old destinies* and bring ourselves into new possibilities. I will not try skydiving only because I have not done it before. Yet I can try a new Indian restaurant, African vegetarian menu, or writing as a career. I have not published a book before until I become 49, but who knows if I can make more money out of it than others?

Did you know that a criminal usually commits the same type of crime repeatedly? I watched a police documentary the other day; one guy was arrested for uploading photographs of minors; the officers unlocked his smartphone and said the guy had five photos again. Later, they found out that he had been arrested for the same crime three times before in the last twenty years; he was in prison for years for similar convictions like child assaults, etc. I guess he failed to go against his own destiny as well.

If we stay in poverty too long, it can attach to our life like a superglue and will never get off; it is important to get out of poverty soon once we are in. I know some always look poor no matter how much they try to take care of their appearances; they look impoverished even in Mercedes or new clothes; especially, their fat never goes away. Before this happens, I think we all should get out of brokeness. **Some never go against their dooms by birth and stay despair for lives**; some surrender to poor karmas and live like slaves.

* * *

There was a boy's pop group in Korea in 2003; it had three male performers. I recall they were not extremely popular, but reasonably famed; probably, they had been on national TV 10 times a year in the 2010s; occasionally, I could see news about them in entertainment sections on the internet.

What was the most unusual about them was the *lead* singer. *Weirdly*, **he was known for his**

exceptional poverty in 2003. I am not sure of the exact reason, but I don't think they made a huge amount of money, to begin with. The news I read was something like this: He could not afford his car, so he had to sell it, finally; it was the hardest decision since he could not be on public transportation as a renowned figure. I remember another article reading that his fans collected some cash in a paper box and gave it to him at the end of a meeting; the head of the fan group said, "Do not misunderstand us." I guess these all happened by 2004 and I forgot about them for decades afterward.

I believe it was 2017 when I found him with a wife and six kids on TV again; I used to watch some family reality shows on YouTube. Then, my daughter was seven years old and I wondered if I was the only one having a hard time raising a child. For that reason, I used to watch American shows like "Jon and Kate plus 8" or "19 plus counting," but I watched Korean programs as well, which usually described the daily lives of large families on screens.

At first, I thought the guy in the reality show was not the lead singer I knew; it was a long time ago, anyway. But, as I watched more than 20 minutes, I realized that it could be the same guy who I remember. After I checked Wikipedia briefly, I found out that it was him! I was shocked: **What six kids?** People who never had a hard time as a head of family won't understand this. And, for the first time, this idea struck me: **Is there anything**

like a poverty destiny? Are some born to be poor throughout their lives? Why do they go back to poverty again even though they have a chance to get out? *He didn't necessarily have to have six.*

I know a few people who never get married, or have only one child since they had hard times growing up in large families. Oprah also once said 70% of black ladies in the U.S. are singles. I think she might have exaggerated it, but I believe about 40% of them are actually single. Still I think that is rational if they believe they have had hard lives all along and do not want to pass them to the new generations without improvement. Population is increasing crazily these days, anyway.

In a sense, the Korean singer blindly sentenced himself to be poor for the rest of his life. The interview showed that his parents were actually upset when they found out that he had the third child in 2011; they worried how he could raise them all. I can understand if he had been wealthy for life, but apparently he had suffered greatly with money all along. Has he been following his "original poverty doom" mindlessly for decades?

* * *

Another example is Lupe, a Mexican girl who I used to know at work. I think she was about 22, studying at a community college and working as a CNA at the nursing home in 2018. She was chubby, had a tattoo on her lower back and had some taste of luxury goods (e.g., high end wallet). She said that she was originally born in Chicago, but her parents got divorced when she was a baby. So she had lived with her mom as a single child, but her mom passed away when she was in early teens. Her father remarried and has three sons in a new household, which is stupid from my angle. As a result, she had three step brothers, but lived by herself except getting little help from her father and relatives. She had lived most of her life in South Chicago, which is the most dangerous neighborhood.

Her social media showed that she met a fat Puerto Rican boy, with a spider web tattoo on his neck, in her late teens. They rented two rooms on the third floor of an old house and the rent was less than $500 a month in 2018, which was less than half of the average one-bedroom apartment rent[7] in Chicagoland then. The boyfriend looked tough, but could not get any job or help her much with money; who was useless from a financial point of view. **I guess that all these had been a "*given* hardship" for her so far**; she was in a substandard situation, but I guess none of these had been her fault by 2018.

To everyone's surprise, she gave birth to a son out of the blue in 2019; it was a shock since everyone didn't even notice she was pregnant. Even more astonishing

---

[7] $1,200

was that the baby was a black boy although her fiancé living together was a *white* Hispanic from Puerto Rico. It seems he did not realize this until the baby became a couple of months old. She used to post photos of the baby and her boyfriend napping together or having a good time on Facebook. But I saw that the guy unfriended her one day and completely disappeared: **I think he finally realized that the baby was not his.** In 2020, she abruptly posted a photo of her newborn daughter again. Seemingly, she got pregnant again right after her first son was born. She wrote on social media that finally she got one prince and one princess or something.

Apparently, she found a new boyfriend who is the father of the daughter: A young Mexican guy without hair, but with lots of mustache and beard. I could see that she will have a hard life. The new boyfriend's Facebook showed only photos of his daughter, not the black stepson. The situation would be like he will stay with Lupe only to take care of his own daughter, not the step child. **He can act selfishly for that reason in the future**: "I am supporting someone else's child for you." She may have to put up with a lot of crap since he is the one who gives her a favor, technically. I found out that they all moved out to California in 2021. I cannot find her Facebook page any more as I have never made a Friend with her on the site.

Just like the Korean singer, she might have been born following a poverty destiny as well. Statistically, Latinas produce more babies than others in North America. But did she need to follow the tendency because she is one? **She did not resist or even seem to recognize her predetermined destiny.** She added two children already in her hard situation and made sure to be more penurious than before. All I remember is that she had troubles paying rent and complained about them repeatedly even before having her first baby.

* * *

I guess that this concept of "going against destiny" worked out somehow in my case. Most don't know this, but Koreans drink way more[8] than Americans in general. If you visit Korea, you can see way more bars and "room salons (karaoke bars with prostitutes)" dedicated to alcohol consumption. Not only there are more places, but the types are diverser for the poor to the super-rich in the nation. **Personally, I do not drink or smoke at all.** I have never stepped in a *room salon* for life. Do I have to follow the popular trend only because I was born in Korea? I do not like alcohol by nature, but even if I do, I will never spend on a salon as I heard these are super expensive.

Let me give you the last example with my friend, Joe. Different from Vanessa or Lupe, I actually liked this guy

---

[8] Possibly the most in the world.

and always felt deeply sorry for him. I also found that his case is outrageously unique: **He could have let go of his poverty destiny permanently, but unnecessarily caught it at the last moment.** Joe was about 55 years old when I first met him in 2015: A big white boy with an easy going character; he had a wife with four kids. He worked for two dishwasher jobs every day to reduce his credit card debt (about $30,000) then. His first job started at 6:00 AM to 2:00 PM; his second job was from 5:00 PM to 9:00 PM. It was the second job where I met him.

I was working at the luxury restaurant in the nursing home every evening for only four hours in 2015. He was very tired and leaned himself on the dishwashing machine all the time. The job was hard for me even as a part timer; I cannot imagine how hellish a life he had lived. He was such a generous guy that he always stopped his van whenever he saw me walking. I owned a mint vehicle by 2017, but always walked to work since it was nearby and I didn't feel like it's worth spending gas for it.

Joe said the first job he got was sweeping the streets in downtown Chicago; he was a teenager at that time; there is no job like a street sweeper any more, but we know Joe is old[9]. Then, the first serious real job he got was automobile assembly technician at Saturn factory. Ostensibly, he had been content during those 30 years of

---

[9] He was probably 63 in 2022.

employment. He eventually met a lady and got married at the age of 42. **Even though he married a little late, he ended up having 4 children.** Then, sadly, Saturn filed bankruptcy, which is the reason why we don't see the brand any more. He said his debt had piled up after being laid off from the tech job. He still had to pay a mortgage for his two-bedroom condo and feed four kids on top of it. He landed on a dishwasher job, but had to work two jobs to reduce the debts.

Have you ever been a dishwasher? I have always thought the senior housing kitchen was a hell created by humans: Intensive repetitive labor combined with high stress. Dishwashers are dalits in the kitchen caste from a view; everyone disrespects or bullies them all the time; they seem to live on the Earth like others, but actually go through *hell* every day. Here is a question, though. Joe was not married until at the age of 42: **Couldn't he just let go of the chance to get poorer?** Did he have to grab the last opportunity and produce four kids, so he had to work double?

Joe finally got a heart attack in 2018; which I learned could happen by mental stress as well. I heard he took a 6-month break, got unemployment benefits and came back to the position in the end. I always felt he might be destined to work to death throughout his life: **Maybe creating four kids would have been a way to follow his destiny solidly.**

My hypothesis is that some people destined to work hard even create drudgery to do so; some are uneasy about having easy lives; a few might even intentionally make themselves poor, so they can work more. They may do it subconsciously, so no one notices it. This is why I believe we need to get out of poverty quickly: Before we feel comfortable with it; before it becomes our fate. Frankly, this has been what I felt about myself, too. Even when I got enough dividends from stocks every month, I couldn't stop working as a dishwasher handling garbage. I even created excuses like "This is good for my exercise" or similar - the truth is that I was not comfortable having an easy life. Eventually, I was afraid this "working blindly hard for no reason" would become my destiny.

Let me add one more example for this predefined destiny before finishing: Kim K (social media celebrity). She must not have been broke, but I assume she might have lived a sore life so far. The bad news is that she may have to continue it for a while from now on; to me, she also failed to challenge her own destiny. We all know that she had repeated break ups countlessly, and then divorced three times as well. Having too many relationships is like having too many wars in a country.

Nonetheless, when she had the wedding with the rapper for her third marriage, I thought she was finally done with all those splitting headaches and would live peacefully ever after. But, to my surprise, she ended up having four kids by 2022. These four kids can bring her whole new set of different problems. I am not saying that her children are bad; I just know what usually happens when a single mom has four kids. In my opinion, she did not have to direct her life that way. More importantly, **I felt like she lived a boisterous life too long, so it became her destiny.** Instead of cutting out stridence, she created more into her life. A new vociferous life can be permanent this time since there is no divorce with our own kids.

* * *

Even if we are born to live loud destinies, I think we can challenge them if we feel these are not good for us. The opposite example to Kadashian can be Paris Hilton in this case. It shows that she got married to a rich guy and has one child in 2023. She may finally have a peaceful life even though she used to be a troublemaker – seemingly, she challenged her original destiny in a sense.

Whenever I lifted heavy garbage cans in the nursing home, walked to work in the snowy winter or rode public transportation to try famous but cheap hot dogs, this question hit me occasionally: **'Why do I live like this?'** I thought, 'Am I supposed to live poorly in this life? Is this the reason why I am living stingy despite all my savings?' The fact was I have had more than enough for over a decade, then. 'Maybe I had lived beggarly too long, so I cannot cut it out?' One day, I decided to quit the nursing home job and become a writer in 2022. So far I am much happier since I can work less hours for writing – not like laboring 13 hours a day for dishwashing. If this self-publishing works out fine, maybe I can make more money than before, too.

In summary, I am glad that I had the chance to help the elderly for almost 7 years. But it had been painful that I knew I could not do it forever: I do not think we should continue our lives blindly only because we have lived that way for long; we should not be afraid to be different from our own folks. Furthermore, we should not live by suggestions even though they are from ourselves: **Our wrong destinies can suggest something invalid persistently.** Above all, we should know what we like, what we don't like or what makes us painful. We should think outside the box every now and then – looking at ourselves as if we look at someone else. I am certain that we will make better choices that way.

* * *

Summary

1. Do not continue living your life as before mindlessly.

2. Keep a habit to try something new all the time; it can help us change our destinies.
3. Don't work too diligently unless there is an obvious reason for it.

12

Auto Addiction

70% of Americans do not need to own a car.
-Brad Kong

While I was still working at the video game shop, the owner of Maria's massage visited me one day. She gave me a couple of coupons and explained that these are extremely good deals; I felt desperation in her eyes. I believe she needed to pay rent or something, but no one visited her parlor. I almost thought that I would help her out once, but suddenly didn't feel like it: Why? I saw that she was getting into her car parked in front of my business and it was a mint Infiniti QX80 – the biggest SUV the luxury brand makes! It was over $60,000 in 2011 and her business was permanently closed out years ago.

The famous Chinese actor Chow Yun-fat is known not to own a car; it shows that his net worth is over $700 million in 2022. Japanese stock billionaire Takashi Kotegawa (known as BNF to Koreans) also said he does not own a car in the city and rides a bicycle in Tokyo. I checked their interviews a little more in depth; Chow said he owns one car and chauffeur even though he *rarely* uses them; he rides subways in Hong Kong everyday. BNF said he has one car in his hometown, which is in the countryside.

Virtually, everyone owns a car in America. Even though automobile and gas prices are not necessarily cheaper than other countries, Americans just have one. **People who have never lived outside America do not know how overkill it is.** Imagine everyone in the Netherlands owns skates or everyone has a smartphone in Finland; these are, at least, more cost-effective and less troublesome. It also means that living in America is pricier only because of this "mandatory"auto ownership. I personally have lived without a car since 2017 although I had owned two for 18 years before. Getting rid of my car was the best decision I made in the 21st century; I feel less stressed now.

Owning a car will expand our chances to spend cash, often regrettably. There are mega shopping sites with *free shipping* everywhere these days; major supermarkets started *free* grocery deliveries recently. **I don't think we need a car necessarily to shop any more.** Since we can go to physical retailers by wheels easily, we just end up squandering more, especially during weekends. More importantly, *owning a car itself costs a lot even when we do not use it.* Sometimes, I wonder if auto ownership is the source moving the American economy.

No one can take a break comfortably once he or she owns a car since it bring a good amount of bills constantly.

* * *

I think walking is important since it can develop our brains; scientists proved that it prevents dementia or other mental diseases. I don't think people believe this, but I still can see that I am getting smarter every day at the age of 50: Don't my new books sell better than old ones? I assume brain development continues for a really long time. I remember that I didn't even know how to take the subway right when I was in high school; I didn't know how to read the subway maps. And I see that some people are still at that level of intellectual capacity.

Occasionally, I see people who cannot figure out their passcodes in the libraries: the two digits of our birth month and the last two digits of our birth year; I witness some never figure this out. There was a group of four Mexican families who took the 600 bus straight to downtown the other day. It took 20 minutes for them to figure out how much fares they have to pay for; it took another 30 minutes for them to figure out how to buy CTA subway fares after the bus ride. No offense, but I guess I used to be like them decades ago. I could see that they are die-hard drivers. I am sure there are people who never understand how self-publishing works: **We can be poor, but can not be stupid.** Being stupid may be lethal and we cannot expect to survive that way.

Missing chances to develop our brains is a big loss. The Japanese Brain Institute also strongly recommended walking to develop our brains: "Get off one station earlier on the subway and walk." I am not sure if I have gotten smarter only because of walking; still I realize that I finally understand things that were not clear before. I am the fastest person using ATMs or self checkout machines in a supermarket. Besides, I often get good ideas to write while I walk. **I think that not having a car is a way to maximize our brain exercise while saving money.**

* * *

Americans seem to own too many cars as if they are free; people spend more to live in North America than Asia solely for auto related costs; Americans make similar, if not less than Koreans. Except for calling Uber once a week, my family of 3 have lived just fine without a car in a Chicago suburb since 2017. **While owning a car causes all sorts of problems; it can cost something beyond finances, too.** One ridiculous story I ran into was the case about Sandra Bland: in my opinion, she virtually died because she owned a car and was a smoker. From the start, I think people have higher chances to meet police officers when they drive. I read *Talking to Strangers* by Gladwell and it starts with an episode regarding the death of a young lady.

Sandra was a 28-year-old African American from Naperville, Illinois; she graduated from Texas A&M in 2009 and had diverse jobs. In 2015, she was driving to start a new job in Prairie View, Texas and got pulled over by a traffic cop named Encinia. I actually watched the whole footage on YouTube and it seems everything started as a routine traffic stop for a signal violation; the officer asked for license, registration, etc. Then, suddenly things got pretty bad after she started smoking; I assume the officer was a nonsmoker. He asked to put out the cigarette and she refused; they started arguing vigorously; eventually, she got arrested and transferred into a jail. Surprisingly, she committed suicide by hanging in the jail three days after she was booked.

Would she be alive by now if she was a non-smoker? I did not realize that it can cause a death like this. Or would she be alive now if she did not own a car? Are these too much to suggest although officer related deaths were increasing in 2022? I know some people really need a vehicle for their jobs. Yet too many individuals own them habitually for no compelling reasons; there are plenty of alternative choices, but chumps don't consider them from the start; as a result, autos bring a full spectrum of problems into their lives. In finance, a car drains a chunk of dough, big enough comparable only to housing.

* * *

I am not blindly on the police side. In 2003, my girlfriend, who is wife now, and I went to Miami, FL from Champaign, IL by my new car then: the greatest road trip of my life. On the way back from Florida, we planned to stop by Charleston, SC since I heard it is a well known tourism city. Not long after I crossed the SC border, I was stopped by a traffic cop, and he said I was driving too fast. It was amazing that the local highway had a 30 miles speed limit; he said I was driving 45 miles, which is still pretty slow for a highway in common sense; he also explained that I do not have to go to court, but have to mail a $52 check for the fine to the ticket, which was fishy. I felt like I got robbed for nothing.

When I think about it now, these crooks were there intentionally; probably, it was a speeding trap for many first time visitors. It is not natural that I got into a local road with a 30 miles limit suddenly as I had driven all along at 65 miles from Florida. They just chose newish cars with foreign license plates to make $50 easily. Since these low lives ruined my day, my wife and I canceled the Charleston plan and decided to go home directly through Georgia. Later, I heard a lot of Americans complaining about similar experiences. I am glad I did not spend a single cent more in the state and got out.

I believe this lady, Sandra, might have a similar situation as I had. According to the report, the police car was driving fast and pushing itself right behind her car, so she was yielding the lane for it. Then, she got pulled over for not turning on the signal for yielding; simply, this guy stopped her for nothing. It was unfair, but I believe she should have acted a little cooler; I did not tear up and throw out the ticket to the police; I just regret to mail $52 in 2003.

Regardless of this incident, apparently, she had written a lot of articles against the police regarding black rights movements before she hanged herself. I still believe it's better for us to remember these officers are humans, too. Writing more tickets does not bring them more salary, so it is worth being polite and explaining things a little; I do have some experiences where traffic cops did not write me anything and moved away. She did not have to act rudely or start smoking in front of a non-smoker. Or better yet, maybe not owning a car can solve *all of* those problems. **Personally, not owning a car has gotten rid of 30% of my life problems in the last 6 years.**

* * *

The first car I had was a brand new Hyundai Elantra in 2000; I had kept it for 13 years; the second car was also the new Elantra in 2013. Maybe I bought a Hyundai twice since I am from Korea. However, I honestly liked the designs of both models. I kept the second one only for 4 years, though. My car ownership had been 18 years total though I have rented cars before and after.

Throughout the ownership, my biggest horror came from mechanics. Have you heard of "Mechanics trauma?" Probably not as I coined it. Getting ripped off and over-charged repeatedly for decades, I had strange symptoms that made me feel freaked out even with getting the smell from mechanics: The mild gas smell from their working areas. Cars went back from mechanics in worse condition even after spending a chunk of money for repairs. I had to squeeze my budget crazily since I had been short of money. Some mechanics replaced original good factory parts with cheap after-markets even after getting $1,500 for repairs.

I was her.

I particularly had a hard time after my first car became 10 years old in 2010; my daughter was born and economic depression came that year. The store could not make profit, but I had to keep pouring money into my old car while mechanics didn't do much. I should have replaced my first Hyundai by then. Monthly payment for a brand new car could have been cheaper. For some reasons, I thought it is wise to keep an old car with healthy repairs. **Honest repairs improving my car never really happened throughout the 18 years.**

* * *

I was in college when I bought my first car in 2000; it had been great for about 7 years. The first frustration came after the *timing belt change* in 2005. The old Canandaigua dealership said they will give me a loaner and asked me to leave my car for a day for repair. They suggested a strangely lower price of $375 even though $500 was common then. You know what? **They did not change it.** In 2005, I was about to finish up college in Buffalo, NY and planned to move to Chicago to start a business permanently. I thought I will visit NYC one last time since I just got a new timing belt, anyway. After parking my car on a street in Manhattan, it did not start again. I spent $2,500 on towing, getting a new timing belt and replacing the damaged cylinder. It took a few days to repair in Manhattan. I had to come back to Buffalo by bus and flew back to NYC via JetBlue to pick it up. I estimate the total damage was over $3,500.

Horror from mechanics did not stop there. In fact, it was merely a start. Whenever I went to any car related place, I spent a chunk just like nothing. I felt like American solid consumption starts with car ownership. Once we have it, we must spend a good amount of money somehow. Even a low life's favorite excuse to ask for cash is "gas money."

As a result, I live in a walkable neighborhood now. Though our neighbor, Jim, had lived without a car for 30 years, I thought that it was crazy to live without it in the beginning: How can I, right? **I guess we are all addicted to cars to some extent.** I used to have chronic back pain when I owned the store; that was long gone after I started walking exclusively. I am much thinner and notice that *I have more free time as well.* It takes time to wash, clean, maintain, fill gas into or repair a car; I do not have to visit the DMV, insurance office, police station or court, either.

* * *

How can an ordinary citizen be a criminal quickly? I think driving a car makes the chance ten times higher. Drinking at a bar and coming home is not really a crime. With a car handle in our hands, it is. Good people can be hit and run criminals; maybe some are not just good at driving. I used to rent a car every month after removing my car in 2017. Renting has become less and less and almost none now after 2022. My wife calls Uber about once a week.

When I worked at the store, there was a nice, but poor maintenance guy working for the plaza; Bogdan was Polish, had three daughters and *four cars*. He had two jobs and his wife worked full time as well. Nonetheless, they had been flat broke all the time. Later, I learned that he lost his house via foreclosure in 2014 though they had paid a mortgage for it over 20 years. It is sad to see that a man lost a home while keeping four junks guaranteed to drain cash out of his family. Humans have lived with a car for over 6 million years. One car a person is wasteful, toxic and unhealthy – *this does not happen except in North America!*

* * *

Summary

1. It's not necessary for everyone to own a car.
2. 30% of my life problems have been gone after I sold mine.
3. It has been and will be manageable to live without a car thanks to IT advancements.

13

Pointlessly Expensive Educations

There is a difference between education
and high spending on tuition.
-Brad Kong

I have an odd hypothesis that *moderate* success can actually be harmful. I am not saying that we should not try hard. But, theoretically, I think it's better for us to be successful completely or just fail. One example of such a mediocre success can be a dentist. If we are totally good at studying, I think we should go to medical school with a scholarship. Or if we are not good at studying at all, I think we may just start working early; some build up wealth faster that way. A dentist is in the middle of nowhere: They were neither extremely good at studying nor academically bad enough to give up studying.

Dental schools are notorious for high tuition; some graduated with over $1 million student loans. Yet they make far less than MDs. There are so many dentistries in America that virtually every strip mall has one already (our town square crossing has six). As a result, the dental practices are ill-famed for overcharging only to make their ends meet. I have got swindled by one, so maybe that's the reason why I am writing negatively about them. Even so, I think this could be an example that **a little bit of success can hurt us more than no success at all.** I think I myself have wasted a lot of time and money only because I had studied just above average.

I have wealthy parents, who are divorced. Unfortunately, I have not had an amicable relationship with them for decades. Thankfully, they gave me some money after my daughter was born, so I was able to buy my condo, which I believe has been the best investment. Although I have had a healthy amount of savings all along, I had chances to manage an unsuccessful business and work in low income jobs to compensate for the loss. I have been in a position to observe both the rich and poor closely.

I believe that writing can be a way we can truly live forever. When we think about famous people throughout history, we can see that half of those are sorts of writers. Even among kings or queens in the past, some tend to get more famous when they had written something: Aurelius, Caesar, Napoleon, etc. There have been famous painters or composers, but these art and music require highly trained skills. I believe writing is the most realistic way for ordinary folks to leave something before passing away. Most of us just focus on making a little more money during our lifetimes and die. *Making more money than we need can be a waste:* **Financial gain but life loss.** From a perspective, writing after school years can be a true way to start thinking without worrying about grades or tuition.

* * *

Truthfully, I think some may be poor since they are not smart enough. Here is good news, though: Not every genius is born that way. I strongly believe that people can be more intelligent as we make an effort toward it. In other words, most clever people are made: **Being intellectual is achievable.** What kind of people make more effort for it? People with stronger survival instincts.

There is a difference between being wealthy and smart: Being wealthy can be rather temporary, but being shrewd is unstealable. I saw on the news that a Korean company sold a floating liquefied natural gas (FLNG[10]) vessel to Mozambique for $3 billion. Were Koreans able to make it only because the country is wealthy? No. There are rich countries not knowing how to make things. For instance, the GNP of Qatar is often number one in the world. Fake rumor joked that the Qatari sultan gave out super cars to every citizen once, yet we all know that the country doesn't know how to manufacture a vehicle.

There is no TV in my house; the three in my family mostly read books, mostly. For some reason, all the books my wife reads are fiction: Grisham, Petersons, etc. All my daughter reads are kinds of children's diary series: Dork diaries, Diary of a Wimpy Kid, etc; strangely, she also reads a lot of catalogs from *Lands' End* repeatedly. She just

---

[10] A huge gas mining and purification ship.

graduated elementary and is interested in modeling, which is understandable. We had too many of those catalogs since my wife buys from them occasionally.

I never read fiction unless it is a graphic novel; I am more interested in what actually happened in real life and how we can solve any issue if there is one. I am particularly interested in the hardship the poor have to go through in these times: Dickens and Hugo were the same as they wrote *Oliver Twist* and *Les Miserables* respectively. I read Korean books as well, but a lot of books I read are self-helps. It sounds ridiculous, but I read *12 Rules of Life* by Peterson in the Korean version since it is easier for me; I am writing about the book in English, though. I strongly believe *reading is the best education*, regardless; reading habit would be *the most valuable inheritance* that my daughter would get from us.

It is not arguable that education is a key to success. Nonetheless, what I mean by education is *actual processes* of educating ourselves: thinking, reading, writing, going to libraries, etc. Some people, especially those Korean trolls, seem to make the mistake that education is spending on high tuition to get degrees; these are not the same. **In my opinion, true education virtually does not cost anything**; meditation, deduction, discussion, interpretation, translation and realizations are all free. We just need time to be alone.

* * *

I was stupid before I graduated from SUNY in 2006; I had followed the major trend of education blindly, failed and lost a lot on tuition. Probably the biggest waste of my parents' money on me was those English programs for non-native speakers in American colleges. There are plenty of ways we can learn English these days. But, for some reasons, attending ESLs[11] in the U.S. universities were popular in Korea in the 1990s; these were expensive. While most typically attended only one ESL for a year, I have attended three; total periods were about 2.5 years.

- RIT: 6 months (1997)
- Cornell: 1 year (1999)
- SUNY at Buffalo: 1 year (2000)

Probably, wasting on education is better than on others. Maybe I learned more English and western culture; these helped me get a bachelor in America. But these were expensive including room and board; Cornell was the most expensive only because it is a stupid Ivy League. The city of Ithaca was so small that I had felt suffocated for the whole year; I had visited NYC a lot during that era. I was overly stressed out and skipped the classes often, which is unusual for me.

Only good thing was I met my wife at Cornell; notably, she came to the ESL on a Fulbright scholarship, which was rare. After that, she won her master's at University of Ark

---

[11] English as Second Language

Fayetteville and doctoral at UIUC on full scholarship. She has helped me a lot in the last 24 years, including giving birth to my daughter. It is unusual for a man with a bachelor's degree to be married to a woman with a doctorate. Maybe Cornell was worth the tuition after all. Regardless of her degree, I learned that it is extremely hard to find a good woman I can really rely on.

* * *

While I was working at the nursing home for almost 7 years, I was able to win two certificates from two different institutes: Medical Coder from AAPC[12] and Pharmacy Technician from PTCB[13]. Honestly, this was possible partly because I had been a weekend part timer. I had spent most of my time studying at the library by myself.

The medical coder license was called CPC[14] given by AAPC and, luckily, it did not require me to take their online courses, which could have cost me $3,500; they allow people to take and pass their exams without course registration. In 2016, I just bought their official text book for $100. I bought another famous book[15] and other required references (CPT, ICD-10-CM, HCPCS, etc) from Amazon and studied for about two years by myself. The exam fee was $350 for 2 attempts and I passed it on the second try. It was great since the total amount I spent was

---

[12] American Academy of Professional Coders
[13] Pharmacy Technician Certification Board
[14] Certified Professional Coder
[15] *Step by step Medical Coding* by Buck

less than $1,000 to get the certificate. It was good to have a library near home.

In the case of the Pharmacy Technician license, the PTCB required me to take one of the online courses from an organization they approved; there were hundreds of courses and organizations available. At first, I thought it was a trick to make more money out of me: "Why do I have to spend on tuition again?" But it turned out that one online course[16] was only $200 for 5 months in 2021. If we could not finish within 5 months, there was an extension fee of $100 a month, though. I was able to finish it within four months. The course was extremely helpful and I might have not passed without it. The PTCB Exam was $129 in 2021 and I passed at the first try at Pearson center in Illinois.

Private education businesses have been booming especially in Korea now. **Getting a good education is one thing, but spending a lot on it is another.** But, if you have a lot of money like my father, maybe it is the only place we can pour some money in. After all, these are all unique and valuable experiences to me.

* * *

Summary

1. Spending a lot on tuition doesn't necessarily mean getting a good education.

---

[16] RxTechExam.com

2. True education may cost nothing even though it requires hard work.
3. I know one Korean troll who never graduated from a college in America, but spent a lot on mortgage and car loans: *Stupid.* **Still, it's better to waste money on tuition than others.**

14

Not Imitating a Billionaire

*One guaranteed way to get out of poverty
is to imitate a billionaire.*
-Brad Kong

There is one disregarded secret to become rich:
**Reducing the years to pay a rent or mortgage
during our lifetimes.** Average people are less
concerned with money drains, but more with incomes:
This is wrong. I bought my condo in full when I was 40
years old in 2013; as a result, I have not gotten any rent
or mortgage in the last 10 years. Let's take a look at my
housing expenses by age.

- 0-20 years: Living at my parents' house ($0.00)
- 20-40 years: Mostly paying rents except during my
  army service ($1,000 a month)
- 40-100: Home ownership (HOA association fee up to
  $370 a month by 2022)

**It seems I can manage to spend less than 20%
of my life on paying rent**, which had been much

higher than the condo HOA fee. On the contrary, this can be a typical life of a mortgage payer in America.

- 0-20 years: Living at parents' house ($0.00)
- 20-40 years: Rents
- 40-70: Mortgages
- 70-100: Rents *again* (downsizing from houses)

A lot of Americans pour money solely on their houses for decades and end up having nothing else after retirements. Occasionally, they sell them and move back to rental apartments. **In this case, people can spend 80% of their lives on paying rent or mortgages**: *Outrageous drains.* As medicine science develops, it is possible that people can live more than 100 years. Then, it can be more than 80% of their lives from now on.

Ideally, buying out even a small condo *early* and living *without* rent or mortgage for as long as we can sound like a good strategy. Do you know who else took the strategy? Warren Buffett. This billionaire[17] bought out his house with full cash of $31,500 at the age of 28 and has lived there for over 65 years by 2023. **It seems he will conclude to spend only less than 8% of his life on paying rent.**

* * *

---

[17] $117 billion net worth in 2023.

Why do we have to make money? To me, the primary reason is to protect ourselves from suffering. Poverty always brings us *pain* one way or another; it can be a mild or severe pain, which can come to us today or 30 years later. The misery could be something like not having enough for hospital treatment, or working in a hellish job. There are jobs where nine out of ten people quit within a week; still some work there for good since there is no other choice; they curse every day, but still go to work. I think we have an obligation to keep ourselves from going through torture. Most people get more chances to get out of a hell in their early ages and less in late. **But, eventually, some may get stuck in a hell forever.**

A lot of people mistakenly think that getting rich can be accomplished by working hard and saving money: Not true. More important things are luck, ability to figure out and take opportunities, financial knowledge or having some useful connections. **Being wealthy is a combination of multiple constructive things.** Let's take my condo purchase as an example. I had some money prepared in my savings in 2013: Cash preparation was crucial, but everything. I was lucky to have a housing market crash that year and sharp enough to take the opportunity. I knew one real estate agent who is the mother of my friend and she helped me quickly to grab the deal within a day. I knew how to tell a good condo from bad ones within half an hour. I had some financial knowledge to figure out *not having a mortgage is* *supreme.* I knew how to use up a small space to the maximum for my family of three. After all, it was a combination of luck, opportunities, cleverness, decision making, knowledge, skills, connections and cash.

* * *

Being rich and decent are different: I would say that **the noble are less likely to move by greed.** Some may look wealthy, but actually have more debts than others; this is just a result of stupid avarice to own things; they are scapegoats in capitalism and slaves in the lowest block in the personal finance pyramid. Having some control over desires makes us decent. I have one child though I could have five if I really wanted. For whatever it is, I think people who don't do a thing they could have done look decent.

"What is the difference between being broke and poor? **Being *broke* is temporary while being *poor* is eternal.**" As Kiyosaki quoted in *Rich Dad and Poor Dad,* what we may seriously need is an asset, not necessarily a job. According to him, assets are things that put cash in our pocket automatically and the examples are interests, dividends, book royalties, etc. Personally, writing a book means trying to build another asset while I am getting some interests and dividends every month. When I think about it, the best thing my wife did to me financially was introducing the book in 2006; she read the preface to me in a Border bookstore and I wound up buying it. I had a chance to get small fortunes a few times since 2006 and have lived on interests after putting all the money in the bank, accordingly. Without the book, I could have wasted some on super cars or something.

The most controversial concept in the *Rich Dad* book is whether a house is an asset or not: Kiyosaki strongly suggests that a house is merely a *liability*, which means spending; I am on his side. If we are not sure what to do in real life, I think the easiest way is to see what other rich men did and try to imitate them. It shows the net worth of Kiyosaki is over $100 million. He may be more correct than us, moneywise. I am not going to trust some Korean trolls having huge mortgages arguing over this: **I personally believe it is a loss to buy a big house.**

Opposite to Kiyosaki, there are people like Edelman suggesting paying mortgages as long as possible. According to Orman, these types of financial advisors are nothing but *frauds*; they just want your money for a house upfront, so they can use it for their own investments. I see that sales of E's book is hardly ranked within 500,000th on Amazon while Kiyosaki's is high within 100th in 2023.

* * *

I do not want to *waste* my life *pointlessly*: **At least, not for now.** I want to enjoy it with a bit of control since I am not about to pass away yet. I know some

Koreans go to the Philippines or Thailand, and enjoy their lives at the lower costs there; there is no future for them; technically, a majority of them are in the low-income class in Korea, too. We don't exactly make money while we mingle with bar girls or assimilate ourselves to pimps in substandard countries.

There is a travel writer named Park; he is not fluent in Thai even though he had stayed in the Kingdom for more than 12 years; both he and I are 50 as of 2023. I think we are still too young to start looking downward, enjoying little achievements and indulging ourselves mindlessly: I am not saying that we should live *diligently*. I just feel that it is too early for people of my age to start being laid-back by comparing ourselves with unblessed citizens in tropical countries.

It is a good thing to enjoy our lives; I will never work for a job for the rest of my life. Nonetheless, there should be some bottom limits; I do not want to feel proud and relieved after placing myself next to people from Southeast Asia. I may be richer than those from Africa, but can be settled in the low income class in North America that way: We should stop comparing ourselves with people in deprivation. Stop visiting impoverished countries unless you have a specific business. **Being wealthier only because we were born in America instead of the Philippines is not an achievement.** I don't know why I have been interested in Thailand travel lately, but I decided to visit Thai restaurants once in a while instead of drinking in Pattaya for real. It is better for me to have that moment of indulgence and wastefulness *as late as possible*: It is better for us to *delay* a harmful desire if we cannot remove it.

* * *

According to "Outliers" by Gladwell, the richest man ever existed in history is John D. Rockefeller; experts estimate his net worth over $500 billion USD in 2020. It shows that this is what he said when he was alive: "Do you know what the biggest joy is in my life? **Getting the dividend check every month.**" I think I have gotten my stock dividends and bond interests for 12 years now as of 2023. These used to be less $100 a month initially, but over $2,000 a month now in 2023.

I believe the easiest way to get out of poverty is by imitating super-riches. Believe it or not, statistically, most super riches were not born rich: there is a reason why they have become one. We do not necessarily have to be millionaires. **I believe getting out of poverty is more important than being wealthy:** Does it make sense that we can stay beyond the poverty line at least when we copy what billionaires did when they were poor?

The first day I bought stock was in 2011 – $100 of Pitney Bowes; my daughter was one year old at that time. I had worked at the video game store then and made twice more money out of eBay sales than store sales.

Whenever I sell a game online, PayPal lets me print out a shipping label through its site. Pitney Bowes logo was always on the top of the shipping labels. I thought the company would be profitable since millions of items are sold only on eBay every day. Besides, the stock had given out good dividends. After buying the stocks, my interest in investments has grown – I have been particularly interested in dividends since then. **Interest from banks and dividends from stock are basically the same things** while half of stocks in the market do not give out dividends.

* * *

In the 2010s, I was obsessed with Warren Buffett (he was more popular, then). He was the second richest person in America and has been a long term dividend investor. But the Wikipedia article on him helped me in an unexpected way. I had rented an apartment before 2013 and thought I would buy a big house with a mortgage someday. **However, I learned that he bought his house in full for $31,500 in 1958 and still lives there for over 65 years** – I thought it was intriguing.

I had about $80,000 in Bank CDs, which my parents gave me for an emergency. I was interested in a three-bedroom house in Roselle and it was about $200,000 in 2012 – it was after a $100,000 price drop thanks to the subprime mortgage crisis since 2009. But, unfortunately, this means I still needed a $120,000 mortgage to buy that house. No one would have given me that amount of mortgage since my business was not doing well. Even if I got it, I could have been in a situation to pay $2,000 a month for 30 years: **Not the life I have ever imagined.** Strangely, several months later, I was able to find a one-bedroom condo for $60,000 in a different town – a way better neighborhood than Roselle. It was 2013 and the economic depression had stayed for more than a few years since 2009. In particular, condo prices dropped a lot.

Still, this was my concern: 'I have never seen anyone buying a house in full. Do I really have to go for this?' I truly wondered – I was even afraid since no one around me in America did it. I had reached this conclusion in the end: 'This billionaire did it for a $31,500 house. Let me just imitate him. I can move out later if I am not happy. Who knows if I can end up with $10 M since he made $120 B this way.' You know what? It turned out to be a good decision when I think about it now in 2023: **One of the best things I did with money.**

* * *

First of all, this 850 sf one-bedroom condo has turned out not to be very small as I expected. My wife and daughter do not live together all the time for reasons (this is actually true for a lot of families for colleges, travels, jobs, military, etc). Certainly, it is enough for me, but even when we stay together, we reasonably divide the space into three sections: Usually, living room for wife, bedroom for daughter and walk-in closet for me; the walk-in closet is about a room size in this unit. We already have bought enough space-saving furniture from Ikea and renovated this home.

Secondly, since I used cash, I could get a discount on the house. It was originally $65,000, but the owner cut $5,000 immediately for a cash deal within a day. This condo is over $150,000 after having lived here for 10 years since 2013. With mortgages, there is no real discount on any house – often, people end up paying a house price double with a mortgage than cash buyers. Thirdly, I have saved tons of money by not paying rent or mortgage interest.

Fourthly, I was able to sell my car and live a car less life since 2017. Usually there are more facilities around a large condo complex. We have 3 super markets nearby. And I found my nursing home job within walking distance as well later on. I sold my car for $7,000 and have never worried about gas price ever since. Fifthly, condo HOA increases have been much slighter than APT rent or house upkeep increases. I think I have saved about $2,000 every month compared with renters and it has been 10 years.

Lastly, the library happened to be nearby coincidently. I was able to pass two exams for certificates while working at the nursing home for weekends. Even publishing these series could not have been possible unless I lived close to the library. **Benefits have been great only because I copied Buffett once** – maybe there is a reason why he made fortune.

Later on, I learned that Roselle is worse than I thought in the beginning. Library was not close to the house, but it had been particularly small and outdated. And blackouts have been repeated since all their electricity lines are in the sky while those are underground in my village. I am glad I did not choose the single family house in Roselle though it even appeared in my dream once. I still remember that I woke up in the middle of night once from the dream of that house. It looks like a dull house now, but I do not know why I wanted it so badly in 2012. **Maybe not everything I want wretchedly is a good thing;** having a debt with that house could have been a big regret by now.

* * *

Summary

1. Check what financial decisions billionaires made when they were poorer.
2. Personally, the smallest house in town turned out to be still large for my family.
3. Not everything we badly want is good.

15

Being Too Religious

True religions never ask for money.
-Brad Kong

Some countries like Afghanistan may be poor because of the dominance of Islamic zealots like the Taliban; many of them care more for Allāh, instead of making ends meet for their families. I think that most Indians agree that caste social classification, which originated from Hinduism 3,000 years ago, is an obstacle for their economic growth as a whole in the country. I concluded that being religious beyond common sense can be a reason for poverty.

I believe religion was created to benefit people initially. Let's take ancient Egyptians, for instance; I read that some worshiped the God of the Sun 5,000 years ago; "Ra" was the name of the deity. **This makes more sense since all the lives on the Earth grow basically thanks to the sunlight.** When we think about it, we can see that the photosynthesis of plants is the source where all the wealth comes from. In fact, the concept of affluence was created only after people started accumulating crop harvest surpluses; Harrari explained this well in *Sapiens*.

When I was in the Field Museum the other day, I saw quite a good amount of cat mummies in the Egyptian collection; it means they also deify cats or treat them equally as humans at least; this makes sense to me, too. A cat is a unique animal catching and eating mice without touching plant crops; those sparrows and mice have been the biggest problem for farmers for thousands of years; there is no better animal to protect harvests than cats. **It seems what ancient Egyptians did was more reasonable than what we are doing now.**

* * *

The Chinese leader Mao once said to the Dalai Lama that, "Religion is poison." Marx defined, "Religion is the opium of the people." Schopenhauer once quoted, "Religion is the masterpiece of the art of animal training." It is surprising that I agree with these to some extent since I am a kind of Buddhist myself. My mother and wife are Buddhists even though they are in different sectors; I am not very religious like them, but I read books by monks occasionally.

Still, I candidly believe that current religions have been twisted for governors to control low class people; it does not matter which one it is – everything has been utilized by regimes for reasons now. The fact is that so many religions have been created and diminished for thousands of years; there have been so many weird practices as well. It is up to us how we can react to them. In my opinion, the first sign of a wrong religion is asking for money somehow – I think we should be careful if we detect that.

So far, the most cruel practice I have heard is "Sati" in Hinduism from India: I read that a wife used to be burned together with her husband in case her husband passes away before she does. It is not like the widow killed the husband; she just got burned to death together with her deceased husband *for nothing*. Every human can produce productive outcomes, so killing a woman this way is just a waste of the working force in a society.

When a country is poor while its people work hard, there is a reason. I know Indians are industrious in general. No offense, but it seems India has a lot of severe corruption in the country, including the caste classification. This could be the reason why the country seldom wins a gold medal from the Olympics despite an over 10 billion population. Being wealthy is not just about money. **In a sense, wealth tells if a society runs in a constructive way or not.**

I am not very religious, but here are a few things I decided to do for society. First of all, I will be more concerned about the less-privileged; I may not be able to donate much money, but, at least, I can keep writing books about poverty for them; I hope they will read and help themselves to get out of there. I will continue thinking about the struggles and study them to improve our conditions. Second, I can stop eating meat, at a minimum; we can benefit other animals on the Earth more this way. **Personally, I think religious people eating meat are hypocrites.** I have never liked meat since I was a toddler; my mother always tried to feed me some since she wrongfully believed it's healthy, but that never worked out. I hope I can save all the animals from the farms, but that may not be realistic. Most people think about *only humans* when it comes to charity – this is wrong. I hope people will learn that other animals are as important soon.

* * *

Some people are broke all the time since they get too involved in a religion. In my opinion, an average hard worker is not supposed to be broke, especially in America or Korea, in the 21st century. **I read that some people donate all their money to some cult Christianities in Korea.** Personally, I had negative experiences with Korean Churches all along until I left the country. Christianities there are much different (corrupt) from those in America. The only common thing is that they keep the same Bibles in the Korean version in their churches.

Before starting, let me tell you that South Korea has a grotesquely large number of churches crammed, especially in the Seoul area. These are mostly small chapels, but the numbers are unbearably many compared to other countries. I am sure half will disappear if governments charge property tax on them. Good portion of these are nothing but money grabbing sinful organizations.

Similar Korean churches have been even in America for a long time, but they never accept Americans to attend: Churches only for Koreans. Isn't it weird? These have never been a place we can stop by comfortably and pray. In particular, we don't see a black or Mexican there since they assume the poor probably do not have money to donate. *Since fund collection is their priority, all they focus on are advertisements and propagations.* They will ask Koreans to join their parishes crazily, which is a form of stalking I had suffered from. I hardly go to Korean supermarkets, but if I do, these church people are always there, usually around exits. They are like an aggressive form of Jehovah's Witnesses we see in Chicago.

When I was in college in Korea about 30 years ago, there was a church guy who followed me everywhere on the campus. **It was painful for me to be stalked by a man and I learned why stalking is a crime.** He did not care whether I was studying in the library or taking exams. He even checked my exam schedule and waited outside the classrooms. Maybe he hoped that I would give them some money or bring some friends to join their church eventually. Please trust me that these people never contribute anything to society.

* * *

There was a Korean guy's blog I used to visit. He was an IT technician working in an American high school and his wife owned a dollar mart. Coincidently, both happened to be hard core Christians. One day, he wrote that a Korean minister from his church visited their dollar mart on its grand opening day (evening, more specifically). And he continued that the corrupted human being suggested donating the entire first day sales to the Lord (this is why he visited the place at the end of day, not earlier). The stupid guy kept noting that he donated it gladly and was ashamed that he didn't think of it before the greedy minister suggested.

I honestly was disgusted by two things. The evil minister did not care for how hard it is to run a small business. He just didn't miss a chance to make a little extra money since asking for more donations usually works better on the opening day of a business. Apparently, this blogger had trouble with money for a long time, which was the reason why they opened the store. Second, I was amazed how a human can be such a low self-esteem slave voluntarily without having any common sense at all. What did he mean that he should have thought about donation before the shyster suggested? **What did he really owe?**

When I checked the blog last time, the dollar mart had been closed for good only after a few years, which is not surprising. He wrote that he had been packing a lot of stuff at home since it was highly possible to move out from his house due to foreclosure; to be fair, there had been a lot of foreclosures back in 2011. I could not find any posting regarding moving out after that, but I could see that he had been worrying a lot financially in numerous postings.

* * *

Religions definitely help our lives on some occasions. There is a Buddhist monk[18] YouTube channel I enjoy watching[19] and it helped me a lot when I needed some advice and inner peace; he is the one who made me decide to apply for a dishwashing job in the nursing home years ago. When I think about it now, I am glad that I kept the job for 7 years then. The place is nearby, so I have lost a lot of weight by walking to work. I have studied at the library next to the nursing home and passed two exams for certificates: Medical Coder and Pharmacy Technician. I was about to get one more certificate of AWS Cloud Practitioner, but I decided to write books instead.

---

[18] Pomnyun
[19] I am not exactly a Buddhist, by the way.

Before getting the job in the nursing home, I thought there were groups of people doing dirty jobs for us. Now I know that there is no difference between me and them. I guess I have been getting matured by heart – we are all the same weak creatures, after all. Seven years of hardship fixed my arrogance well and I believe this spiritual growth is the biggest asset I have gotten from the job.

* * *

Summary

1. Being religious and obsessed with blind beliefs are different.
2. Some "leaders" have modified religions to take advantage of unenlightened people. If a religious person asks for money somehow, watch him or her out.
3. There is a difference between being generous and stupid.

16

Being Gullible

We don't have to be too nice.
-Brad Kong

In *The 48 Laws of Power,* Greene suggests not to trust our friends *too much.* It sounded weird in the beginning, but when I thought about it, it made sense somehow: *What do we exactly know about our friends?* Technically, they are sort of strangers from other families we happened to be close to. He took the example of Michael III of the Byzantine Empire in the 9th century; this king was murdered when he was 27 by a close "friend" named Basilius[20] in the stupidest way possible in my opinion; he should have not given too easy "chances to get murdered" to his *actual enemy, who was* disguised as a friend.

Michael III was originally the Byzantine Emperor in the mid-9th century (842 - 867); Byzantine was a huge empire then, whose territory included current Italy, Greece, and Turkey combined. Since Michael III became the emperor when he was only 2 years old, his mother and uncle Bardas started governing the country initially; history says that it

---

[20] Basil I

had been just fine for 12 years as Bardas was an excellent governor. Then, the family feud began as Michael III grew. The mother of Michael III interrupted her son's privacy offensively – as a result, Michael III ended up killing a politician named Theoktistos on his mother's side himself and sent his mother to an isolated convent for good.

While Bardas had been the self-controlling statesman, Michael III had been a mere alcoholic living a prodigal life since he was 15; naturally, these two didn't get along very well. The emperor (Michael III) met a person named Basilius on the market street one day and they became close buddies. It shows that Basilius was merely an illiterate refugee with no education; still, he had strong physical power and was good at handling horses. Eventually, Michael III ordered Basilius to kill his uncle Bardas, who was the head of the army then. Subsequently, Basilius became the prime minister replacing Bardas; it shows that it took only 9 years for him to be in the highest position in the empire's military from a humble peasant.

It reads that Michael loved Basilius like a brother originally. Greedily, Basilius kept asking for bigger salary and the emperor doubled, then tripled it – Basilius' power had only grown this way. One day, surprisingly, when Michael III asked him to pay some money back to himself, Basilius refused. It was a wakeup call: **Michael III suddenly realized that this "peasant horse trainer" had more wealth and power than the sire himself.**

The bad news was that Basilius also detected that the emperor's suspicion started budding.

After having binge drinking one night, Michael III awoke and found himself surrounded by Basilius and his soldiers. The emperor's head was cut off that morning, placed at the end of a long pike and displayed to the public by Basilius in 867 A.D. Maybe this was a fair conclusion for a guy who killed his own uncle and placed an unqualified stranger in the highest position: Still, **I feel 27 was way too young to get murdered.** I assume drinking played another major role here as I stated before; the similar assassination was the case of Caesar by Brutus – nonetheless, Caesar (55) died when he was more than twice older than Michael III since there was no alcohol severely involved in the Roman emperor.

* * *

I think we should be careful when we give others a favor. Some people will truly appreciate our help; others may try to take more advantage from that moment. One fat boy stepped on a bus I was on in south Chicago the other day; he was holding a bucket of fried chicken from Shark's and delayed the ride to ask for a free ride to the driver (I cannot believe someone broke that much). The generous black driver granted him, but this boy started eating dinner on the bus, which was uncomfortable and unusual – I was truly disgusted. He knew how to take advantage of others at such an early age; usually, hopeless, bold old people do that. I did not say a thing since I knew he would get off soon before we were getting out of the black area (both the boy and the nice driver were African American). **Getting into a habit of taking advantage of others will make us poor eventually.**

I witnessed that one of the most common but horrible ways to be gullible is "cosigning," especially in Korea. We can get a cosign from our family or friend when we buy a vehicle in America. Yet I believe it's a little different in that country – more *predatory*. Ignorant victims usually cosign any type of debt for others; this is a horrible system to put the cosigner in hell when he or she gets betrayed by the person who asked for cosigning. **I am not sure why those sufferers do it since cosigners don't seem to get any benefit to begin with** – they only take responsibilities when things go wrong. I saw a documentary regarding those victims on YouTube and it was horrid; they put their children in deep misery by doing something they didn't have to do. I saw that many YouTubers posted comments like "*never* ever co-sign anything" unanimously.

* * *

A family of three committed suicide in Wando Island, Korea in June, 2022: father (36), mother (34) and their daughter (10). Technically, it was a partial murder since the police believed that the parents killed their daughter first with sleeping pills. Then, they drowned themselves together in a mint Audi sedan into the sea. The ocean police finally found the car with three bodies inside. The news shows that the father had an incredible amount of debt because he lost a lot of money on a crypto investment called Luna coin. Also, they found the family had lived lavishly driving a luxury sedan despite small income. Conclusively, I would say the debt was the reason for the suicide pact. It was particularly shocking to me since I have a wife and a daughter of a similar age; coincidentally, the girl's name was the same as my daughter; I didn't not know her name was so popular as I see it everywhere in Korea now. The only difference is that I do not own a car at all. Besides, I have never invested in things like coins. Also I do not rent a house like them; I have owned mine outright since 2013.

In general, I would say that the father was merely stupid. First of all, parents do not have any right to murder their child; it is better for us to learn early that our child is a different human being on his or her own. Luckily, I think I realized that when my daughter was only one year old or so; it is too arrogant if parents think they have the right to end the destiny of their child: **No one has such a right.** In this specific case, it shows the deceased girl had "two pairs" of grandparents (from both sides of parents) and plenty of relatives, so she could have survived fine with their support. Besides, when the father commit suicide *alone*, most of the debts disappear *legally* in Korea; I believe that debt is not automatically inherited to the child as long as she give up the entire inheritance from her parents legally. Maybe the father could have sold the car and given the money to the rest of his family before he died: **Stupid people are as harmful as the wicked.**

Coin investments were booming in 2022. I saw Matt Damon say, "Fortune favors the braves" in a commercial. Larry David also made a funny commercial about a crypto trading site. Maybe I should sign up since they are super rich themselves? **These frauds go extreme; they will do whatever it takes to make us hooked.** Personally, I believe cryptos are useless crap; no one uses them in real lives. Some buy *Tesla* stocks only because they seem to be popular; some, including myself, cannot analyze prospectus to see if the stock price is "too high or not;" some buy gold because the news says the gold will go up soon. Some buy coins only because there are people who claim to have made a fortune: Bitcoin, Ethereum, Doge, Mara etc; the credulous don't even care about the types as long as it looks like quick cash opportunities.

I personally have never bought a coin: **Never ever will.** I *usually* buy stock from a company if I use their product, and be happy with it. This gives me more confidence in the company and helps me hold its stock longer, which generally brings me better investment outcomes. I personally believe coins will be recorded as a humdrum hoax in the 21st century (like Tulip mania in the 17th century).

* * *

Financial crimes are getting commoner these days. One of the guys I used to see on a Korean site said that his wife had lost $500,000 through voice phishing. He said those frauds are so skillful that the victims included even a Harvard professor in his case. Though nothing serious happened while I worked in the nursing home, I had been involved with diverse types of receptions while owning the video game store. I am glad I shut it down permanently in 2014: No worries any more. Here is what happened.

First of all, we[21] had a lot of shoplifters. I think I called the police at least over 30 times during that 8 years. Then, we had a couple of identity theft problems with credit cards; probably, I have lost $130 or so for two new games. And I had ATM deposit fraud once. Gladly, Chase covered the $1,000 I lost that day; it was not their fault at all, but they gave me $1,000 cash out of their pocket; which is the reason why I will stay with them forever. Lastly, we had a robbery at a gunpoint in 2009, which was 5 years before I closed out the store permanently.

I believe the gun was a fake during the robbery in November, 2009. At that moment, my pregnant wife was next to me. The robber hit my eyes for no reason and got all the cash from the register. I believe it was about $160 then. This made me wonder if I have to keep the store open permanently or not. Eventually, I decided

---

[21] Actually, it was just me who was the only employee and owner.

not to renew the store lease after that. I had countless ugly customers as well, but let me not talk about it here now.

* * *

When I think about it now, I was a too nice guy when my store just opened in 2006. I did not want to invest $2,000 on security cameras which turned out to be extremely necessary. I had been the only employee for a long time until my wife came to give me a hand from 2007. The store had been in vulnerable condition the whole time.

Before opening the store, I had 3 months of free rent. That was solely a trick from the cunning landlord; his real job was a lawyer and every tenant in the strip mall did not like him. He took one month of security deposit in his pocket when my 8 years' lease was finally over in 2014. So it was like I got two months of free rent, but I spent that for store set up and construction. The rent was $1,200 a month in 2006. I think I spent about $30,000 including game purchases for the meager opening in 2006.

Do you know who came first as soon as we opened the store? A customer with cash never came for a long time. I could not make any sales in the first 10 days until Javier Martinez, who was a great Mexican boy, came. But, strangely, a lot of people still came and these were mostly sales people, advertisement ladies, job seekers, shoplifters and other potential criminals. They all came to take advantage of the "Cyb Knight" somehow. While most people were great and tried to help us, there had been shysters always trying to take advantage continuously. Besides, I learned that corruption in non-profit organizations was severe as well. I got trillions of calls to the store phone asking for donations and learned that many actually put 90% of collections in their pocket and gave only 10% to the poor.

* * *

As far as donation goes, I guess I will just pay enough taxes, instead of giving money to a charity; governments help poor people with their collected taxes, anyway (i.e., free or discounted housing; food stamps, coupons or SNAP cards; Medicare, Medicaid, etc). **Focusing on paying more or enough taxes should make my spendings simpler** than creating a foundation in case I become rich. Besides, I do not have to worry about an audit when I pay more than enough taxes.

There was a lady named Pippa Bacca in Italy. I read that she tried to cross Europe via hitchhiking to show how the world is safe in 2008. Twelve days after she started this "Brides on Tour" project, she was found dead in Gebze, Turkey; she was 33 years old. Justly, it shows that the rappist, Murat Karataş, was caught and had a life sentence in prison in 2012. We can be good people. Yet I don't think we need to be too nice beyond a reasonable point. World can be a harsh place to many and we can end up being dead when we insist on our ideality and interrupt others.

* * *

Summary

1. We can be nice. However, we don't have to be too kind.
2. Frauds do extreme things to deceive chumps.
3. We have an obligation to protect ourselves first before anyone else.

17

Giving Up a Little Too Early

A miracle can happen; it may need enough time.
-Brad Kong

Giving up can be wise depending on the situation; one efficient way to get out of an addiction is stopping trying or delaying. There is a popular Korean posting site called Dcinside[22]. I used to write a lot there and became a minor celebrity by 2009. After all, it turned out to be pointless for me to write more at a point; the trolls there started offending me in diverse ways (e.g., making prank calls to my game store, etc). Still, it was hard for me to quit writing all at once since I had millions of fans. How was I able to quit though? I always thought I would check the site *a little later*: **Delaying was the key and worked out fine for me**; I haven't been on that site since 2009.

Nonetheless, there are people getting incredible losses from everything since they *gave up too early*. For example, the Jewish writer Anne Frank, who wrote *The Diary of a Young Girl*, passed away when she was 15 in

---

[22] Similar to Reddit in America.

Bergen Nazi concentration camp in Germany in 1945. Surprisingly, it shows that she could have been saved by the English troops if she managed to survive only a few weeks longer. There is a group of *young but fat* women in Korea; they call themselves feminists, but Koreans call them twisted feminists[23]. Coincidently, I notice that many in this group are obese; celebrities representing them are plump, too. Regardless, from my perspective, they seemed to *give up* on themselves too early; they gave up on being pretty; abandoning their bodies to be in whatever weight is merely a sign of their neglect, which is from losing hope. I honestly do not believe that they can be happy even as singles.

* * *

There is a company named CVR Partners (ticker: UAN); it makes nitrogen fertilizers for agriculture. I bought 120 shares for $10.30 each in 2015; it was a great *dividend stock* then and I spent about $1,235.00 to buy those. The bad news was that the stock price dropped 90% out of the blue in 2017; even worse was that the company did a 10-to-1 *reverse split*. **As a result, I had only 12 shares of that stock with a 90% loss for five years since 2017** – to break even, the stock price had to go over $103, which seemed to be impossibly high (after reverse split, 120 shares for $10.30 each became 12 shares for $ 103 each). **It had been a failed investment for 7 years since 2015.** I just did not sell

---

[23] "Maegal" in Korean

those off since there was no point. Then, all of a sudden, a miracle happened.

The price of this UAN stock suddenly jumped up to $107.25 on 1/18/2022. It was way over $103, so I sold all and made +$52.82 profit, conclusively. All I heard was that fertilizer could not be imported from China due to some trade disputes that year. Which was why this U.S. fertilizer company stock jumped up. I am glad I did not give up too early and sold them all for 90% loss; waiting for 7 years after the purchase of the stock had been too long, though.

Lately, the novel titled *Pachinko* written by one Korean author has been a big hit and a series of dramas based on that book was released by Apple TV. I read that the book describes life stories of four generations of Korean immigrants. I thought my life story is as good as theirs and I can write an epic chronicle about my life once. **I made a small fortune (+$20,000) out of PBI stock in January, 2021** and let me tell you what happened.

I

There is an American technology company named "Pitney Bowes" in Connecticut, USA (ticker: PBI); which is best known for an online postage machine called "SendPro." After we sell an item online, we can print out postage with this machine and drop the package at the post office. Simply, that machine had made my online sales much easier. I had invested a lot of money in this company from 2011 to 2020 – I had owned a $65,500 amount of 6,300 PBI shares by 2020 ($10.40 each share). I had bought PBI stocks little by little whenever I had chances for almost nine years.

I thought this company had a bright future: Online sales had helped my retail store from the start all the way up until it was closed in 2014. I opened my shop in 2006 and we had made used items sales on Amazon, eBay, Half.com, etc. **Before PB made the delivery tracking system** integrated in PayPal, which is connected with eBay, **keeping USPS tracking numbers on receipt papers was a hassle.** Before 2009, I had to go to the post office and wait in line whenever I sold an item, mostly on eBay. If I chose to use certified mail at the office, they used to give me tracking numbers on green receipt papers. After selling dozens of items, I didn't even know which tracking number was for which items, exactly.

The biggest problem was fraud buyers. There were the dishonest, who lied to eBay or Amazon that they did not receive an item. These companies ask sellers to provide tracking numbers showing proofs for the deliveries. If sellers could not find the exact tracking numbers on papers, they took money out of sellers' accounts. A lot of amateurs stopped selling online for this reason until 2009.

This happened to me a few times as well, but **I just did not have the luxury *not to* sell online.** I invested so much in the retail store already in 2006 and it did not do well all along. Store rent was relatively cheap[24], but the location did not bring us enough foot traffic. You get what you paid for, right? Still, I had good feedback on eBay and Amazon, so I was able to make more sales throughout 8 years: Often online sales were twice bigger than store sales. However, the problem with fraud buyers remained until 2009.

After Pitney Bowes invented the electric delivery tracking system for online sellers, I did not have to worry about those frauds any more – its software lets me print out postage on my own printer while saving the numbers in my eBay and PayPal[25] accounts automatically. The tracking numbers have been saved together with items sold on eBay after 2009. I could easily provide tracking info to eBay by clicking a link next to an item, so disputes were resolved quickly in my favor. Besides, good buyers have been able to check delivery status easily as well. Tracking is a natural part of online purchase these days, but it was innovative back then; inquiry emails about delivery status have decreased dramatically. That was great for time saving since I had to work by myself in the store most of the time.

---

[24] $1,200 a month by 2014

[25] eBay and PayPal were basically the same company since PayPal was spin-off from eBay in 2015.

I remember that I sold a lot of my items particularly on Amazon from 2007 till 2008. Then, I used the *Stamps.com* service with a $15 a month fee. I did not like the site very much since they upgraded software once in a while for any reason and it made my computer freeze unnecessarily. Yet I remember that the PB software in eBay had been always working smoothly; besides, it was free with eBay sales (no subscription fee). **As online sales literally saved my store, I thought every retailer needed it someday.**

I invested originally $100 for this company in 2011. PBI was one of S&P 500 company stocks until 2014 – it came with the highest dividend among S&P 500s as well (up to 12% a year at one point). I probably invested up to $30,000 by 2015 – I finally ended up investing $65,000 by 2020. While this stock had always come with dividends, I was at risk of losing -$40,000 in 2020 since the company did not do very well, particularly after 2015. It sounds ridiculous, but that was the reason why I ended up owning so many PBI shares by 2021: **I had bought more shares simply because the stock price had kept dropping every year.** It is called "averaging down" – some buy more shares when a stock price gets cheaper. An average purchasing price of a particular stock can get *lower* this way.

Let us say that we bought 100 shares of A company stocks for $500: The average purchasing price of the stock is $5 a share ($500/100 shares = $5/share). Then, let's suppose the company did not make a lot of profit, so the stock price dropped to $3. If we buy 100 more shares, our average purchase price becomes $4 now: We have 200 shares of A company stock with $4 average cost a share ($500 + $300 = $800 and $800/200 shares = $4 a share). Sometimes, I think people do this when they have faith in a company: "The stock price will go up to $20 someday. I will make more profit by lowering the average purchase cost now." **I did it because I believed I could get out of loss at least by lowering my average purchase price**.

* * *

I remember the Pitney Bowes did just fine until 2014; PBI price was up to $28 then. I mistakenly believed that I was a visionary investor (the next Warren Buffett). I was too optimistic and invested about $30,000 on PBI by 2015. But when the stock price dropped to $12 in 2016, all I hoped was getting out of it without loss. **I was desperate and bought more shares whenever the price dropped continually**; *it was risky since we can lose everything if the company files for bankruptcy;* some commit suicide because of the reason. $65,000 was huge, especially to me then.

The CEO Lautenbach came to the company in 2012 and the company stock price had been downhill since 2015. Apparently, the tracking system was invented long before he came. I can see that he is still the CEO of the company as of 2023. I personally do not understand how he has managed to keep the position in the last 11 years: I heard that he gets high approval rates with votes at the annual stockholder meetings. PB has about a $600 million market capital and hires 10,000 employees. I absolutely have no idea about how politics works there. **All I know is I had miserable five years before 2021.**

I checked a lot of information while I was suffering from the loss. One thing I noticed was the CEO still had gotten paid $ millions of salary including benefits a year despite the long loss: I thought he got a lot of wage considering the stock drops. His salary had been $1 million a year and the huge benefit had been added on top of it; he is certainly not the type of a person willing to get paid $1 a year like Jobs or Trump. **Nonetheless, astonishingly, I ended up making +$20,000 profit mainly thanks to "Wall Street Bet[26]" from Reddit,** but it could have been a big time loss that I would never be able to get over for life.

While the stock price had always been in a downturn, it got ridiculously low after Covid pandemic hit in 2019 – PBI was as low as $1.69 in 2020. I understand most stocks crashed in the beginning of 2020, though. Since

---

[26] I finally wrote "Thank you post" on them in 2022.

PBI was up to $28 in 2014, it had been over 90% gradual drop for the 6 years by 2020. **However, miraculously, I ended up making $20,000 profit out of selling all the PBI shares** – all the 6,300 shares on 1/26/2021 (Tuesday): I remember that it suddenly went up to $14 in only for two days (1/26/2021 to 1/27/2021). This was even more fortunate since PBI went back down soon and it is only $3 even now in 2023. This is the key point: **-$40,000 *possible loss* (2020) Vs $20,000 *actual gain* (2021)** – this is a $60,000 difference! *I am glad I did not give up one year early*; which I believe could have happened if I didn't choose a dividend stock[27], to begin with.

* * *

When I think about it, everything started with opening the video game store in 2006. Then, incidentally, I happened to watch the news about an old lady in Lake Forest, IL; her name was Grace Groner and she left $7 Million as inheritance to a school when she died in 2010. It shows that she bought only three shares of ABT stock in 1935. **It made me interested in dividend stocks.** Along with the news and several financial books I had read, my business put me into PBI stock purchase in 2011. Whenever I sold an item on eBay, the shipping postage label showed the Pitney Bowes logo on top. Without eBay sales, personally I would have not known about PB – it's

---

[27] PBI always has given dividends.

like my online sales brought me +$20,000 capital gain and an extra +$8,000 dividend income from PBI.

Why did buying a dividend stock, instead of just stocks, play an important role for my gains? To begin with, I think it is crazy to buy a stock without a dividend when there is one with it. We need some safety nets in investing: Dividend incomes. I suggest people address stock investment as if it's a savings account, especially for beginners.

II

As I mentioned earlier, I graduated from college in March, 2006. Then, I had been a power seller on eBay since 2003. I received a Bachelor of Science in biology with a 2.6 GPA, so I chose not to go to graduate school. Instead, I decided to relocate to Chicagoland to start a business since my girlfriend, who eventually gave birth to my daughter, studied for a doctorate in Champaign, IL. Before leaving Buffalo, I sold virtually everything in my apartment via Craigslist; it wasn't hard since new college students were looking for used furniture or TV to start the new semester; a Ukrainian girl contacted me and brought some cash with a couple of her friends; I remember one of her friends was a biology instructor at UB.

After finding a new apartment in Rolling Meadows, IL, I moved everything from Buffalo to there on Elantra. I felt the place was a little expensive[28] while the size was also bigger than I needed. However, I did not have much choice since I didn't know anyone in the Midwest. It was cold in March and I needed to find a place quickly. I did not rent a U-Haul though it is over 500 miles between Buffalo and Chicago – I wasn't sure if I could drive a big truck for such a long distance; I did not have much cash left to spend on renting a truck, either.

So I used my car twice to bring everything to Rolling Meadows from Buffalo. I brought my cat on the second trip; he was tired in his cage and slept through on the backseat during his 10-hour trip. I had back pain for about two weeks because I had to lift too much heavy stuff. I bought a new kitchen table from Meijer and assembled it for my new place. I bought a new mattress as well and brought it myself by car to save some money on delivery charge, too.

I was all by myself and did everything on my own for decades. I have been through hardships even though I have wealthy parents – I cannot imagine what really poor people have to undergo. I remember that I saw a Mexican lady moving a broken down car on her own on a busy Arlington road once in 2009; she pushed hard, but her car moved so slowly. Maybe these types of things motivated me to write this series.

---

[28] $900 a month in 2006.

* * *

The apartment looked fancy initially, but turned out to be bad since the cunning management raised rent every year while I detected mice inside – my cat caught a few. Besides, their rent did not include any utility at all. It is not that they raise rent because of inflation - **they do it because tenants prefer not to move out once they settle;** not only is it bothersome, moving costs a lot, too; every landlord is a little deceptive in that sense. And this is why we have to buy out even a small condo in full no matter what, instead of going for a bigger house with a mortgage. Unless we own something completely, unpleasant deceptions will never stop; we keep leaking money until we get rid of rent or mortgage.

That complex had window stickers for resident cars. It was my fault that I did not take it seriously, so not to attach it – it had plenty of spaces to park, anyway. But the stupid Redmon towed my car out of the blue one night. **It was immoral since there was no assigned spot in the complex;** the company did it only for money[29]. When I visited the apartment office the next morning, they had no idea of who towed what overnight. I spent $100 totally only to pay for a taxi and get my car back. The taxi driver had a hard time finding the towing company, strangely; he was a middle aged man, but

---

[29] $65 in 2007.

definitely a novice driver. Navigation was not common in 2007. He said it is OK, but I paid him since he tried hard.

I remember that it took about two months for me to find the suitable location for my store – "Loopnet.com" was helpful. I drove around everywhere in the beginning of 2006, but soon I learned it was pointless; an empty retail space is always available somewhere; I just did not know which one was good. I read *The Complete Idiot's Guide to Starting and Running a Coffee bar* then; **it gave me the idea of compatible businesses**: "We should open a business near related ones, so these businesses can help each other; we cannot open it in the middle of nowhere." I ended up opening the game store right next to an internet gaming cafe. I feel sorry for Borders bookstore as I had to return the book after reading since I was too broke.

In May, 2006, I opened my business at a local strip mall in a Chicago suburb; a lawyer owned the strip mall, which was valued about $5 millions; it was huge, but in a slow location. Every tenant didn't like the owner, yet I have to admit that the management suggested the lowest retail rent[30] in Chicagoland. **Without it, my business would not have survived for eight years.** My rent once dropped down to $1,100 a month in 2012 when the management allowed Jazercise to move in right next door. The business made an incredibly loud noise for aerobics, which was abominable. The three woman owners were

---

[30] $1,200 a month by 2014.

frankly the most stupid I have ever seen. They made only noise, instead of money. They charged very little subscription fees to members, but never had enough exercisers for five years. They only made enemies, not a profit; I was 39 while these women were in their 50s.

* * *

My gracious mother gave me $30,000 initially to start up my business in 2006. She has been wealthy, but too generous for her two stupid sons. I got two months free rent out of a 3-year lease contract and spent most of the fund to set up the store. I had no idea about wholesalers, but luckily found one within driving distance – it was a sort of miracle since America does not have that many video game wholesalers. My business saved a lot of money by not paying for delivery charges since my wife and I always pick up new games on our own.

I thought that I would make a lot of money out of refurbishing used games if I could get a reliable source for used games – a small store! It can be a marketplace for customers to trade used games before buying new games (i.e., GameStop). I knew I could make more profit selling used games than new ones on eBay. The size of my store was about 900 square feet, which was right next to DMZ internet café where a lot of guys gathered to play PC games (e.g., *World of Warcraft*). The cafe was eventually closed out in 2012 and I suddenly saw a huge decrease in foot traffic to my store. I still feel grateful to Eddie and

Lance who founded and owned the gaming place. Not only were they great neighbors, they were great customers, too. Eddie brought his uncle and nephew to my store and they bought several video games: Usually Nintendo DS Pokémon series; I visited the Sushi restaurant his parents owned to give them some business. I truly appreciate that we had some more profitable years thanks to him.

Basically, this is how we made profit in our store. We sold new games, accessories and consoles for little gain; the profits were no more than 5% for new items, which was similar for all the game retailers, even for super stores. However, the difference was that we accepted used games, accessories and systems for store credits; customers traded in used stuff and got discounts on new items they bought. **After cleaning used stuff, we sold them for much higher profits, often *online*.** For example, we made about $7 profits whenever we sold a brand new Xbox 360 or PS3 game by 2014, which we got for $51 from a Elk Grove wholesaler; we usually sold them for $57.93 + tax (which is $63 after tax) even though most others sold them for $59.99+tax – we sold $2.04 cheaper than Walmart or Target, not to mention GameStop.

Some pointed out that it was ridiculous we were selling things cheaper than even big corporations. Yet I thought that it was fair since we paid less rent and had no advertisement cost – we had customers' visits only via word of mouth. We had coupon magazine ads once in 2006, but these turned out to be a complete waste: I hate the Indian Pizzeria neighbor who suggested too strongly that. I am not sure if he got any monetary gain out of the referral, but it definitely caused loss on me. **I made up my mind to spend those few hundred dollars on item discounts, not on ads;** I did it until my store closed out in 2014. Personally, I just did not feel comfortable charging the full $59.99. The strip mall had a low income apartment complex on the back. I think I was nervous that we might lose regulars if we charged in full. Still, we did not see a lot of customers since the store location was a bit invisible and obsolete.

* * *

How did our store credit work? Suppose that there is a new game selling at $60. If a customer wanted to trade in one used game, we could value it for $10 store credit if we could sell it for $15 on eBay ($5 profit). Then, the customer pays the rest $50 by cash for the $60 game; it is like a $10 discount on a new game. It was similar to GameStop, yet there were three differences. First of all, *we suggested way more credit* than those corporations. With careful calculation, I concluded that we do not lose money even if we give out enough credits. Especially when they buy another used game, instead of brand new, after trading their own used games, we made the maximum profit. It was better for us to just keep the reputation of generous credit by giving out a lot, **which was an advertisement itself.**

Secondly, we did not have a cash option for trade in: "More credit, but no cash" for used games. Simply, customers could not sell games for money while they could use them for more credit. That was the *best store policy* I had ever made since those street craps fighting for more cash disappeared magically. Before that policy in 2007, there had always been arguments about cash amounts – pointlessly tiring. More importantly, the store had kept losing a lot of money by giving out cash before 2007. **After setting up a "store credit only" policy, haggling disappeared and cash drains in the store stopped as well.** I noticed that we ended up welcoming more quality gamers, too.

Thirdly, we sold refurbished games after cleaning, not just used games. We had two Azura disc cleaning machines – one in the store and the other at home. Azura used to manufacture DVD cleaning machines with price tags up to $10,000. We had two of the $600 machines and provided $1 disc cleaning service, which was popular. We always cleaned used discs, replaced dirty cases and sealed them with plastic shrink wraps; these looked like new. We sold those as refurbished, but the prices were the same as used in other stores.

I still remember one of the worst customers we had was a Nigerian man; he was a middle aged short guy and had strange habits to haggle for aggressively low prices and returned all for full refund in a couple of weeks; he gave me headaches. In the return case, customers only can trade in those only for credits, but he insisted his way. One day, I re-wrote all the store policies and posted it on the wall only for him. I almost called the police on him, which could have been the first time I called them even though no one stole anything: What a shame on him. **I visited his apartment only to ask not to come to my store again** – it is a great shame since most stores try hard to get more visitors. "What kind of monster are you since the store owner begged you not to come? Why do you cause this much trouble in a trivial local store?" I lived in an apartment close to my store then and he lived in the same complex.

I am still not sure of what his job was, but he obviously had a small income with large expenses: Two kids, two cars, two-bedroom apartment rent (which was much higher than my one-bedroom), smartphones, etc. I never understand this type of person: What is the point of having an argument to see who is going to call the police first at a game store? Then, I told him that I will call the police if he does not walk away; he said he will first for the buyer's right. Why didn't he just walk away and save his meager wage on buying games? What is the point of going through all that confrontation to spend money? Probably, he still lives in that low quality apartment with a huge rent now. If rent is a waste, his larger two bedroom rent is a bigger waste – no cure for these types of idiots.

III

PBI was the core part of my investment disaster in 2020. I was on the verge of losing about -$40,000; conclusively, I had four painful years from 2016 to 2020. **This could have been my first major loss if a miracle did not happen in January, 2021.** I have lost money before, but none of it was vast. Currently, I have 72 company stocks and 40 company bonds[31]. I think about 10 companies from my portfolio had filed bankruptcies, whose total loss had been less than $8,000 in the past decade. Now I am getting about $30,000 only in dividends and interest a year, so the loss has not been colossal to me. But losing $40,000 from only one stock could have been substantial.

Before 2020, I have bought most stocks for 100 shares, which is the reason why the loss has been little. In 2020, my situation was like I would be thrilled if I could get my $65,000 back without a loss. **Instead, I got $85,000 back**, *including +$20,000 profit*, from the PBI sales on January 26th in 2021: Do you know what happened? The site Reddit has a subgroup called "Wall Street Bet;" it shows over 14 million members are there in 2023. What I heard was that these investors had united all their trading powers and focused on buying and selling certain meme stocks for reasons I do not understand completely; sometimes, they call it "pumping" or "short squeezing".

---

[31] As of 2022.

One day, they seemed to decide to emphasize on buying PBI, out of the blue. I am not sure why they determined that as I asked around and found no one knows why. The $5 stock then suddenly went up to $14 only for two days, which was supernatural to me. I could not believe my eyes when I checked the graphs that day: "What is going on?" I was relieved for a moment, but I had to make a quick choice: "Do I have to sell all the PBI shares now or wait?" **Fortunately, I sold all the shares as soon as I saw the profit hit about $20,000.** It was 2:30 PM in Central time, which was 30 minutes before the market closed. I would have not made that settlement unless PBI had been a headache to me for over five years.

Above all, **I am glad I was not overly greedy that day;** I happened to confirm that my decision was correct a couple of days later. Soon enough, I saw the PBI went down back to $5 ranges and it has been like this in the last three years ($3 in August, 2023). I am glad I did not give up on PBI too early when all my friends and trolls advocated selling it; they said there is no hope and I could get $0, which means $65,000 loss. **I am glad that I stuck to my own idea.** Simultaneously, I am glad I did not hold on too long when I saw a chance; I thought that a $20,000 profit was plenty, especially considering it was a five years old headache. I do not want to blame the company or the CEO as it is over – I do not plan to buy it again. I just like to thank *Wall Street Bet* once again and wish my best luck to all the members.

IV

Here is a question: Did I make money only because I was patient? *No*, **Absolutely not.** I strongly believe the secret was that I bought "dividend" stocks, from the start. **Dividend from stock is like interest from savings at the bank** – interest and dividend are basically the same things. I would say that only the names are different, primarily. When a stock gives out a dividend, it is called *dividend stock*. Only difference is that banks give out interest every month, but stocks give out dividends usually every quarter (three months). **Not every stock is a dividend stock;** usually about half of stocks in the entire markets are, although this rate changes all the time. These are the examples of dividend stocks: Apple, Pfizer, Wal-Mart, Intel, AT&T, Target, Microsoft, etc. And these are non-dividend stocks: Tesla, Netflix, etc.

Personally, I only buy dividend stocks and ETFs. If a stock of the company I am interested in does not have a dividend, I buy bonds of the company, instead: Google (Alphabet), Amazon, Berkshire Hathaway, etc; these have reasonable interests. **Bonds give out interests, which is the same as dividends from stocks.** In my case, if a company does not have a dividend stock or bond giving out interest, I just do not buy anything from the company (i.e., Facebook). *Why are dividend stocks important?* To me, investment is like we are putting money *that could* *have been in the bank* into stocks. Suppose I bought $1,000 of "A" company stock. **I could have put that $1,000 into a bank and gotten interest every month safely** – no reason to risk losing that in the stock market.

Alternatively, if we buy dividend stocks, we get dividends as if we already put money in the bank; these are often bigger than bank interests, too. For example, Annaly Capital stock (NLY) gives 11% dividend a year while bank interest is just 4% a year nationally in 2023. Since the dividend is like 3 times bigger than a bank interest, I believe it is worth investing in the stocks risking money. Annaly is the biggest mortgage REIT[32] in America and considered relatively safe. If we can buy NLY at low points, **we can make money both out of stock growth and dividends**.

Some argued that non-dividend stocks are growth stocks and better than dividend ones – these are idiots. A stock which is growing is a *growth stock*: **Not having a dividend does not guarantee a growth;** for example, Apple stock has been growing the fastest lately, but it does have a dividend. I notice that usually the poor bet on stock prices without considering dividends; it is well known that the rich are more likely to go for dividends.

I could not have endured five years of loss on the balance sheet of PBI without getting its dividends (5% a

---

[32] Real Estate Investment Trust

year). **I gave PBI enough time for price recovery since I am getting dividends, anyway.** The $65,000 I put into PBI would have been in a bank to give me interests; instead, I had gotten dividends. Technically, there was nothing I had been losing only because of the PBI price drop; I did not have any plan to sell it as long as I got dividends. **While I had gotten dividends, the stock price jumped up for one day and I made +$20,000 capital gain, too.** Sometimes, we need to give enough time to a miracle, so it can find a way to us. I strongly believe it is the right approach to put money into dividend stocks as if we do in savings. At least, we should do it with most of the capital unless we are gamblers.

V

An odd idea hit me one day: "What will happen on the Earth 500 years later? People will not even notice that I existed once." **I guess that I did not want to become oblivious completely.** I thought I could at least record some of my own stories, while I am still alive. On top of it, my desire to get out of the hellish kitchen in the nursing home got stronger in 2021. There was one short Mexican sous chef giving hard times to everyone; he was merely a low-paid cook after all, so I could ask him to bring my food if I saw him outside. The other problem was management interrupted me moving forward to a better job inside the facility.

I had the medical coder license, but they never had an opening for that job for years. I had the pharmacy technician license as well, but the small pharmacy in the building was owned by a different company Symbria and they did not have an opening, either. The kitchen I worked at had kept preventing me from transferring to the server department – they all tried to use me only for a dishwasher. **Not only is this unfair, but illegal** – *I felt like I was trapped in a bad swamp* there. The dishwasher job was way harder than the server's even though both get paid exactly the same[33].

Luckily, I have been in a situation to get enough dividends and interests every month: about $2,500 a month. My wife has been working as well and I have only one child to support. **I thought I could try to be a writer since it gives me more meaning.** People may find my book on a shelf at the library 500 years later and learn that I had existed once. I thought it is better to start early before turning 50; I can still have 50 years left to write if I live until 100. Who knows if I can make more money with writing?

I did not plan to publish a hardcover in the beginning. It was not in my interest to charge more to readers. However, I found four reasons why I may keep publishing a hardcover as well with eBook and paperback. **First of all, there are readers who prefer or even buy only**

---

[33] $16.24 an hour in 2022.

hardcovers. I always buy paperbacks mainly because it is a little cheaper. But we do not know everyone's preference and I did not want to lose a reader for that reason. **Secondly, I learned that hardcover books last longer.** Unbelievably, I found that books have lifespans and it shows that hardcovers can last about 50 years while some paperbacks last 20 years.

Thirdly, expensive hardcover prices make paperback prices look cheaper. I know it is not my primary concern to get profit out of publishing, but I hope some readers buy my books. I think they can buy my paperbacks with less resistance this way. **Fourthly, I can use up my ISBNs.** I bought 100 ISBNs since they offered shockingly discounted price[34]. I am not sure if I will end up writing 100 books in the end. Maybe I can use one more for a hardcover version when 100 is too many. FYI, we need two ISBN for a hardcover and paperback respectively in publishing.

* * *

UnBrokable* in the 1st preliminary series was 713 pages and some may wonder why I try to write a thick book. When I checked Amazon's top seller list, I noticed that a majority of them are thick books. For example, *IT* by King is 1,150 pages. I am not a famous guy - honestly, I don't think I can write way better than others for now. Still, **I thought I could write more than others, at**

---

[34] 1 ISBN was $125 while 100 are $575 in 2022.

least. In a sense, my life has always been like this. I had never shown any excellency in a field or achieved a superior goal. But I think I have worked more than most others, at least. If this series is successful, the reason why would be simply that I have written more than others. **I am good at doing more things consistently over a long period of time.**

Talent may be important. Yet I believe luck can come to a person who tries harder. Readers may choose a thicker book not only because they can get more knowledge, but they know the writer has tried harder. Maybe that is why I have enough savings to support my family without working at a relatively young age. It is 2022 and the news said that a lot of people started coming out for fun even though 300 people die a day of COVID. I still stay at home waiting for my fifth vaccination; I don't think it is over until it is. I suggest not to give up too early or jump into a conclusion too fast: **A little patience can make a huge difference.**

* * *

Summary

1. I had PBI stock and sold all for +$20,000 profit in Jan, 2021.
2. If I sold all the shares a year earlier in 2020, I could have lost -$40,000.
3. Do not give up too early.

18

Preferring Stuff to Money

Buying more things is like getting more pain.
-Brad Kong

In my opinion, **the best way to quit a bad habit can be stopping spending money.** When I think about it, all the bad habits cost money somehow: drinking, smoking, taking drugs, gambling, etc. On the contrary, a lot of the good habits do not really cost any money: meditation, eating small, losing weight, sleeping early, walking, etc.

I think it's important to have an asset account to deposit our experiences: An *experience account*; we do not deposit money in this account, but deposit new experiences. What I mean by a new experience is not necessarily an expensive one. Visiting a foreign country may be a new experience. But going to a different restaurant can be a new experience, too. Even if it's the same brand cafe, we can try to go to the one in a different location. Or we can try a different menu, at least. I have always tried to save money no matter what for life. But I guess that I have only half of my life left, so I decided to spend some from now on – more specifically, I decided to let my money go a little easily as long as I can try something new. In my opinion, there are a few reasons why we have to keep depositing new experiences in the account.

First of all, this habit of trying something new helps us not get stuck in a doom forever. I witnessed that some had worked for dishwashers for 30 years; it's harder but lower paying, yet they had been too comfortable with it; they may never change since they were 60 years old already. **If we keep trying something new by habit, we may have more chances to get out of a bad job, too**: A cook at least in those cases. People may get out of a terrible relationship more easily as well this way. I am not saying that we have to change things frequently – it may be more important for us not to get stuck; a habit of trying something new can help.

Second, this collection of new experiences can make our lives happier. One psychology professor said **it's essential to have diverse experiences to increase our happiness.** There are things we will never know unless we try it; there are clothing we never know how it looks on us unless we actually have it on. Our life can get better little by little as new experiences accumulate, which can make our life more diverse and colorful.

* * *

I have a weird theory that **we can experience more heavens when we stop spending money**: Once we stop, lives get simpler; consumption makes our lives more painful, complicated or disorganized; it eats up time, too. Stopping spending is like traffic clearance for finance – sometimes, we need to wait half an hour or so until there is no traffic jam on a highway. It was medically proven that fasting is good for our health; some do *intermittent fasting* even when they have plenty of money. I suggest that we should not spend money "a day a week" for the similar reason; we have to give ourselves breaks from paying; it would be great if we can make it a lifetime habit. Regardless of finances, it can make our lives more pleasant.

I think it is a waste to spend more time on working to make more money than we need: **Life loss but money gain.** This is what a Buddhist monk said: "We own everything only temporarily; in a sense, we *borrow* everything only until we die." Some people misunderstand that they can still own things if they can pass these to their offsprings, which is a mere *mistake*: Our children are not us. They may appreciate our inheritances, but I guarantee we do not own them through offspring; our grandkids may not even know the correct spellings of our full names. People spend a lot to buy things more than they need; some even get debts for those and waste their whole life to pay them off.

I have always thought that "preferring money" to things makes our life simpler, which can make us wealthy, too. We would not feel ripped off by saving money, at least: In fact, **a little affection for money can be beneficial for life.** Suppose that there is a man trying to quit smoking only to save money. He is addicted, but he loves money too much, so he decided to quit: Isn't it better for our health as well?

There was an actor named Paul Walker (1973-2013). When I checked his profile in Wikipedia, I was stunned that he and I have more than a few in common: He was born in 1973 when I was born; he studied Marine Biology while I have a Bachelor of Science in biology; we both have only one daughter. But there was a difference also: He died from a sports car accident in 2013. Actually, I was astonished that the Porsche totaled was the exact model I was interested in: Carrera GT; I even like the same color, which was mouse gray. Again, I wondered if **there is such a thing like the same *astrological fates.***

Nonetheless, let me suppose that Paul really loved money and went stingy – getting interest out of a portfolio was the biggest joy in his life. Is it possible he would have not owned the supercar from the start and did not get into the accident? **No spending, no sports car and no accidents?** It was not Paul's fault since he was in the passenger seat during the accident. I see similar types of cases everywhere: *Not spending money can save us from a lot of troubles.*

* * *

When my wife used to study in Champaign, IL, I visited her by bus once while I still studied in Buffalo in 2003. We got bored, so we decided to go to St. Louis by rental car. I remember we had a big fight out of the blue near St. Louis that night; she finally got out of the car and walked into a late night restaurant in the suburbs. I followed her and had to order an expensive menu (which I did not enjoy) only to stay there with her for a while. I assume that a lot of stress, including spending on the unnecessary trip, accumulated and sparked up that fight. **What if we stayed in Champaign since we were stingy to save money?** Probably we would have not had it. I believe that a reasonable love for money can make our life actually better – any type of consumption can bring us a sort of trouble to some extent.

Oddly, I do not think that not having enough money is a huge problem – spending can cause more problems. **If we can live as if we do not own money, it can even save our lives.** I read *The subtle art of not giving a f*ck* by Manson the other day; it starts with stories of Bukowski, who had been considered the *laureate* of lowlife in the dirty realism. As I researched more about him, I learned that the poet and I have more than a few things in common – I almost felt like I am him without his fame; drinking and smoking habits.

1. **Both he and I started writing careers in our late 40s.** Bukowski became a full time writer at 49 and published his first novel titled *Post Office* at the age of 51 in 1971.

2. **Both had worked for physical drudgeries for a long time.** Bukowski worked in the post office for more than 10 years. I borrowed his first novel, *Post Office,* from the library months ago. I learned that the post officer's job is extremely hard, overall. I did not know that they have a time limit to finish all the deliveries, which makes the job even harder. I also felt that life had been generally tougher in the 1970s than the 2020s. I often thought that the dishwasher was exceedingly labor intensive since there was only one washing place for five restaurants in the nursing home; tons of dirty pots and dishes were gathered from everywhere. Before that, I had been through other dull fatiguing jobs: Convenience store clerk, kitchen helper, military soldier, banquet server, online sales packers, etc.

3. **Both have *one* daughter, inherited a small fortune after 40 and have been immigrants.**

Nonetheless, I found out that we have major differences, too.

1. **Bukowski had been a heavy alcoholic and chain smoker**. I just don't see a single photo of him without holding a beer bottle or cigarette. On the contrary, I have never been a drinker and smoker for life – one *main reason* was to save money since I had been broke for decades.

2. **I bought out my home 23 years earlier than him.** It shows that Bukowski bought his first house with a mortgage at the age of 58 in 1979. I bought my condo in full at the age of 40 in 2013. Bukowski used a mortgage although he paid that off within five years (super-fast); nonetheless I became the outright homeowner 23 years earlier than him. I remember I got my deed right after cash payment.

3. **Bukowski had to pay child support.** It shows Bukowski had been married twice and had to send child support every month. It seems he had struggled because of it, especially in the beginning of writing career.

Sadly, Bukowski passed away when he just started being recognized – he died at the age of 73 in 1994. As a late starter, he finally started making steady income only from the 1970s and suddenly died of cancer. Couldn't it be better for him to spend some fortune while living a little longer? It takes forever to be a successful writer and living until 90 could have been *possible* without drinking and smoking.

And why does "buying out my own place" *early* matter (even if the size is small)? **I can use the rent or mortgage money for something else "right now."** Bukowski lived in the Carlton Way apartment for 5 years before buying first house in 1979. Google shows that the rent starts from $1,900 a month there in 2023; I am paying $367 HOA[35] a month now: *Isn't it better to spend this extra $1,500 a month on something else now?* Who knows how long it would take for my books to be known? What if that never happens? I don't want to be hungry now and become filthy rich later, especially a little before I die. I want to enjoy my money now – at least, I do not want to suffer financially.

* * *

As a matter of fact, Bukowski's story inspired me greatly in 2021; he published his first novel at 51 while I turned 49 that year. I wondered, 'Can I start writing as a full time author like him?' I resigned from my job since a new company Morrison took over the dining department in 2022. They refused to transfer me over with the same wage rate, so I quit. I could have applied for other jobs, but honestly, I realized that I didn't want any of them; there had been bad bosses or coworkers in

---

[35] It has been up from $279 to $367 in the last ten years.

all, somehow. Worst of all, no one will even recognize how much I sacrificed myself for jobs after I die. **With publishing, I thought I can finally have a chance to leave something.** It can be meaningless for me to work painfully and vanish in 50 years as if I have never existed.

It must have been hard for Bukowski to find a publisher in the 1970s, which had been true for all the writers; it must have been a hassle to write with a typewriter. Things are easier with Google Doc and Amazon KDP these days; I do not even need an editor thanks to Grammarly. I thought that I could try to write a book at least once and have written 30 titles by 2023. I assume that Bukowski's life could have been easier if he was super-stingy: "I want more money. Let me quit drinking and smoking." Then, he might have not gone through divorce or cancer. **Preferring money surprisingly can make our life better than we have imagined.**

Records show that he claimed to have $90,000[36] in his hand by the time he made the first contract for his novel in 1969. I read people thought the claim was probable since he got the money out of selling his father's house and had been frugal. That was a similar case with me. I got some money from my father and bought my condo when I was 40. I think "Buk" could have bought a residence faster if he didn't drink or

---

[36] It could have been about $500,000 in 2022.

gamble. The public deed recorded that *Buk* bought his first house for $80,000 in San Pedro in 1979. If he didn't waste the $90,000 bequest, he could have bought it in full without a mortgage. **Then, he would have been 18 years slower than me, at least**; he was 23 years slower since it took years to pay off his home loan. I think that the poor get poorer in a downward spiral.

I recommend that we should put all our money in dividend stocks and savings accounts – live as if we do not own any money. We have to see how long we can live without spending. After our refrigerators are empty, we may start losing a little bit of weight, which is considered healthy. Then, I think we should try to get as much dividend and interest as possible: **Life paying interest can be hell, but getting interest can be heaven.** I already have over $600,000 in a stock portfolio and get $30,000 dividends a year as of 2023 – it is like I have a job paying me without working. I prefer to keep my finances this way, instead of buying extra stuff bringing me headaches.

* * *

Summary

1. All the good things often do not cost money; bad things usually do.
2. Not spending money for a while makes our lives simpler - do it one day a week.

3. Buying out a small condo in full can be better than a big house with a mortgage.

19

Keeping a TV

Having TV is like spending money
to watch their advertisements.
-Brad Kong

Lately, I read *The Cafe on the Edge of the World* by
Strelecky; more than 4 million copies of this book have
been sold and I found that it has a strong message:
Commercials convey false info that "buying stuff will
make us happy." As a result, people buy more, need
more money and work longer – **a vicious cycle
inevitably ruining our lives.** How do people get
most commercials?

TV is the center of the universe in many households,
which is never a good idea: Especially in consumerism,
TV is a well-designed temptation machine – keeping
nudging us to buy things. If we are short for no apparent
reason, I think we should get rid of the TV first. We can
save on electricity and have some quiet time as bonuses
– we will feel like ourselves again and have sane minds
back finally. **Getting rid of TV solely means we
cannot watch it on a big screen TV** usually in the

living room; my wife and daughter never had a problem watching it on their iPad, smartphone or Chromebook – which still helps me attain quiet time since they use a earphone or headset.

There is one thing we must learn when we read books: Patience – we cannot finish everything quickly. I am a slow reader myself and not necessarily trying to be fast; we all have our own speeds to understand things. *Knowing it takes time* is a great virtue in the age of rushing: **Not everything can be done easily, conveniently or instantly**. The richest man in the world is Elon Musk, according to Forbes 2023; his brother said he grew up reading two books a day. It's also said that Warren Buffett spends hours a day reading five newspapers and corporate reports; Bill Gates is known to read over 50 books a year.

If we are serious about getting out of poverty, I think we may just need to read more after getting rid of TVs. I know it is overwhelming to make such a change to some – most of us probably have watched TV daily for life. But what can we really lose? We can watch TV online anyway; we only save on electricity, cable subscription fees or TV costs themselves. Maybe we can save some eye doctor fees by less frying our eyes on screen. **Most importantly, I think we feel sane, be ourselves and realize where we are again.**

* * *

Nothing is more important than peace of mind. The worst part of TV is it makes us buy more things by bombarding us with direct and indirect ads – the more we buy, the less peace of mind we will have. Our wallet will get thinner while we feel more comfortable when we sit on sufficiency. Personally, I have virtually stopped watching TV since I was in high school; I ended up not going to the movie theater, either; these will only fry my eyes. I believe that quitting screens and sugar are similar; one is for the mind and the other is for the body.

Focusing on a screen is hard work in a sense – continuous night labor after our day jobs. We may finally realize how tired we have been after turning off all the screens. The last time I had a cable TV subscription was 2008. I still have the old CRT TV[37] in mint condition which I bought when I opened my game store in 2006. After that, we used to connect a Blu-ray player to it by 2014; it kept giving me intolerable headaches, so I eventually had to sell it on eBay.

Then, I have had a peaceful life and passed two onerous exams while studying mostly at home: Medical Coder and Pharmacy Technician. My daughter's grades from elementary have been noticeably up after my wife and she moved back into my place in 2018 – wife said she used to get poor grades when she lived with her grandpa who owns a TV. Eventually, my writing career

---

[37] It has been connected to PS2 for 8 years.

has taken off and completed 30 titles so far after my exhaustion stopped and meditation started.

* * *

While I still worked at the video game store, my mother visited me in my apartment in Rolling Meadows in 2007. She stayed for about a couple of weeks and I ordered cable TV for her in case she would get bored; I remember she watched the home shopping channel a lot. **When I think about it now, the channel order was a total waste.** I saw that she played with my cat fine even though she never had a pet before. She could have had a full rest for the first time in her life.

My father watched TV a lot when I grew up. He has been a self-made millionaire all along since the 1980s. Typical among old Koreans, he never had any hobby costing money; his generation really started everything from the rock bottom after the Korean war from 1953. They know what real famine was like and it is impossible for them to spend any money only to enjoy their lives. Naturally, watching TV has become their sole hobby: **Only 3 channels had been available nationally in Korea until the early 1990s, which were free by air signals from antennas.** I was born in the 1970s and lived with him only until I graduated from high school in 1991. The house had two TVs in the living room and the master bedroom of my parents.

My brother watched a lot of TVs, too. But, for some reasons, I have never gotten into that habit. In fact, I hated it when everyone else watched the TV in the living room while I was forced to study alone in my room; they pumped up the volume, regardless – my parents should have gotten rid of TVs, instead of getting me an extra tutor for my academics. **As a result, they lost double on electricity and tutor fees.** Since they kept threatening me to improve my grades while interrupting my study with the heavy volume from TV, they ended up making me a complete enemy – *I haven't seen them for decades now.* They were total idiots in that matter: rude, stupid and thoughtless. Maybe my adolescent trauma is the reason why I live without a TV – I do not want to repeat what they did to my daughter.

* * *

We are living in an era having too many screens. By that time my family was fully into TV when I grew up, there was nothing else – *No Internet by 1997*; TV and movie theater were the only screens. However, the internet suddenly came out when I was in college; there have been too many media hurting our brains since then: PCs, laptops, tablets, smartphones, HDTVs, iMax theaters, Digital Dolby system, etc – there are more things to watch every day. Even TV used to be simpler – now hundreds of cable channels are not enough, so some order Netflix or other streaming services for extra fees. On top of that, I can borrow new DVDs at the library for free or at a RedBox for $2 (2023). There are too many devices showing too many screens to watch – no wonder I feel out of my mind all the time. Currently, I only have a 16 years old CRT TV in mint, which I keep as an antique; this can bring me $10,000 in 30 years. I have already wasted a large portion of my life only on the internet; we get more ads through all these media and end up spending more while getting broke.

Watching the media is like working for another job – physically and mentally, focusing on screen is a labor and many don't get paid. While I don't own a TV, my family has a desktop, two notebooks, one iPad and three smartphones. My wife has a strange habit of carrying her iPad everywhere, watching CNN. We had an argument the other day since she lost her mind again; she did not understand my letter to a government agency; she thought it's for my previous job. I shouted, "Why do I make an effort to write a letter to my previous job which I quitted two weeks ago? I don't care what they do." She clearly showed severe symptoms of confusion: **She did not get heavy exhaustion from working** – she got it from watching the internet.

It is a long story, but I do not borrow a DVD from the library any more, which is free. I used to go to the AMC theater with my daughter every Tuesday since the ticket was only $5 that day – we used to watch a lot of animations together. I think I have been burned out by watching too much media – I hate those headaches after watching a couple of movies in the theater. It happened after watching Blu-ray movies as well. **I concluded that it's nonsense to get sick after spending money.** I got a new desktop in 2022, but decided not to download *StarCraft II*. I used to play "I" a lot when I was in college and even *II* is *free* now. So there is no TV, games, DVD, theater or social media other than from now. These days, I mostly borrow books from the library and listen to audiobooks from YouTube. I can save money, but saliently, I enjoy some time to think alone.

* * *

If a TV is an advertisement machine, I think corporations should give one to us for free. However, most of us just buy it at a high price voluntarily, which will maximize our shopping desires – as a result, we get poorer while we do not notice. A lot of IT giants provide an email or social media account for free. YouTube shows videos without subscription fee as we are watching their ads. I heard Nazi used to provide free radios, so German citizens could listen to the addresses of Hitler every evening. **Modern slaves do not think that way;** they buy pricey flat HDTVs willingly out of their pockets. If you go broke for no obvious reason, just remove it completely out of your life.

See if you can make some time to think alone quietly – keeping a sane mind brings solutions. In real life, I don't think any book can precisely help us unless the author is in our shoes – *it won't happen since the writer is not me.* All of us need to figure out a specific solution for our unique situation ourselves: It's time to turn off devices and start warming up our brains.

* * *

Summary

1. We can get rid of the big screen TVs; we can still watch plenty of TVs on small screens.
2. Media interrupts us from keeping sane minds.
3. TVs could have been free since we watch their advertisements for corporations.

20

Traveling in Too Expensive Ways

True travel is to our minds.
-Brad Kong

There is a psychology term called *anchoring effect*: A cognitive bias whereby an individual's decisions are influenced by a particular reference point. **In other words, a ship does not move far away from its anchor.** Suppose that you drove a Mercedes decades ago and now you drive a Hyundai; you may feel miserable since you are driving a cheaper car now. However, assume that you used to ride a bicycle, but now you drive a new Hyundai; you may feel proud since you are driving such a shiny, expensive motor vehicle. Depending on where we place an anchor, we consider the same car cheap or expensive.

There are a lot of people visiting Thailand or the Philippines though I have never been – many, especially Koreans, visit these for prostitution. In my opinion, visiting those may not be such a good idea, especially when we are young. **Starting to assimilate ourselves to the poor in impoverished countries early won't**

help us financially. We can end up settling in the bottom class in our home countries – for example, white can die as a WT in Canada that way. On the contrary, if a Korean visits only Europe during adolescence, I believe he or she has more chances to stay in wealth later on; we may start comparing ourselves with enlightened Europeans, subconsciously; we may go in that direction throughout our lives. We do not have to try to go low while living uptight is not necessary. Alternatively, I think we can start visiting poor places as we get old.

I used to dream of living in France, Thailand and Peru for a year each. I stayed in Korea for 26 years of my life; now I have lived in America for 24 years. So if I stay in America for two more years after 2025, I will be staying in both countries for 26 years each. I thought it would be great if I could find another country to live in – which is not related to Korea or America. **I thought that it would make my life more interesting.** Personally, I do not prefer very short trips; I favor staying at least a year in a country. Apparently, the problem looked to be language barriers.

Nonetheless, I have changed my mind a little lately. I heard *repeatedly* that Frenchs are arrogant and discriminating. Some Koreans complained that a waiter did not take orders even in upscale restaurants, which is not acceptable as I had been a server myself. I know it has art museums: So what? I am not going to take art exams for the rest of my life as school days are over. I have been to the Art Institute of Chicago a few times with my daughter. Frankly, I didn't particularly enjoy it. If you disagree, see if you are brainwashed somehow.

In the case of Thailand, I heard that the weather is hot and the air is severely polluted. I assume northern Chiang Mai may be cooler, so I hope that staying for one year would be possible long later; in fact, I heard one month's stay is getting popular among Koreans. I like to visit Peru for one year as well, but the high crime rate would be repellant; it is hard to keep one year's expenses safely in South America.

For now, I guess I will just go to French or Mexican restaurants occasionally; unfortunately, I cannot go to Thai any more for dental health. I guess I will go to museums nearby as well, especially when they are free. Oddly, I am eating a lot of Indian thali these days; $7 thali at Ghareeb used to be my favorite. Yet I noticed that, if I spend a little more, I can find plenty of quality thalis on Devon Ave. Regretfully, I do not have any plans to visit India soon. I guess visiting eateries could be a cheaper and safer way.

* * *

Honestly, I don't think I will ever immigrate to a country less rich than Korea; I do not want to travel to dangerous restricted countries, either, as visitors are murdered there. I read on the news that there was a

Korean law student visiting a slum in India after passing his bar exam, and being robbed and murdered – I cannot find the specific case on Google any more since it's inundated with too many similar cases. Some stupid Koreans go everywhere now and their governments keep spending tax money to get them out of hostages.

I watched videos interviewing white expats settled in Thailand the other day; they mostly didn't look good and some planned to move back to their home countries even after staying decades. I detected most didn't look normal – super tanned, unhygienic and hardly spoke out of exhaustion; they acted like drug addicts. While our appearances say many things, **I don't think it makes sense to live in poorer countries than our own,** to begin with. Some tried to build a business, but it must have been harder in a country having less capital with a language barrier. It only makes sense when Thais move into wealthier nations in Europe or North America.

I strongly recommend not to travel to poor countries, at least when we are *young*: particularly Thailand, the Philippines and India – three *broke* wanderer's *popular* destinations. Whereas India is definitely different from the other two, we don't have to start our foreign experience looking downward on impoverished countries. I realized that tourism in the Southeast often suggests *consumptive* pleasures – beach partying or enjoying superficial things at low prices. I think it's better if we *initiate* our world travels as a learning experience;

museums, art galleries or historic sites in once prosperous states. **Where we set our viewpoint at early ages can affect our finances throughout our lives.** I saw some Koreans living poor for life after frequenting poor countries. Also, Americans who retired in Thailand are often blue collar workers. Do not visit poor countries without a purpose; do not go to Siam for bar girls, massage parlors or hotel stays. Alternatively, I think we can do that *after we get old*, at least. People may not see much difference in the beginning, but may see a huge difference later in their lives.

* * *

Thais are known to have lavish lifestyles – this country does not have harsh winters. I found a Korean guy settled in Thailand after marrying his Thai wife on YouTube; the couple sold "Korean churros" in a flea market, but they drove a brand new SUV. **No churros seller can afford a car in Korea;** rich Koreans would not even eat the food they were selling, not to mention cooking it for living; I felt they had a luxurious spending style, considering what they do for living. What is the real reason for men to visit there? Probably prostitution. I know that not everyone does it. Nonetheless, Thailand has had the reputation of the world's red-light district for long; it has an astonishingly higher HIV infection rate, and has been the major port for HIV import to South Korea.

In the case of the Philippines, the Kopino problem has been peculiarly serious; Kopino is a child having a Korean father and Filipino mom. **A lot of low-income Koreans went there for nothing (i.e., gambling), made babies with a Filipina and ran away.** Recently, I watched an impoverished boy selling peanuts on the street in the Philippines on TV; the reporter asked his nationality as he looked different from a typical Filipino; he answered that his father is Korean. It would be sad if my son lived like that. I didn't know the Philippines is just a four-hour flight from Korea until I checked on the world map recently.

In the case of India, we have to admit that it is environmentally unhygienic; I heard still millions of people defecate on the street due to the lack of sewage systems. I suspect that the main reason is government corruption. I have heard that a lot of people, especially Koreans, complain that they felt unpleasant after mingling with Indian people. I had similar experiences; some act as if they are in the high class in caste and I am in the low – nonsense since I am not even from the country. I used to have great respect for India since it might be spiritually high at least.

But, after reading about "Sati", I have a different view – sati is a custom of burning a widow alive in the funeral together with her deceased husband; it used to be common until banned by the British in 1829; horribly, it is said that it is still rarely performed. I do not believe no other country has this kind of custom and it shouldn't be encouraged anyhow. I have never imagined that the UK is necessarily beneficial, but I believe she is absolutely right in this matter. Still, Wikipedia reads *"bride burning* custom has been recognized as an important problem in India, accounting for around 2,500 deaths per year as of 2004." Bridal burning is another type of horrible violence, which can be a mild form of sati or probably has evolved from it.

* * *

While money is not everything, if we keep visiting poor countries, a poverty mentality can stick to our life and never come off. **Koreans visiting poor countries are from the bottom class in Korea.** I have not heard of the super-rich visiting the Philippines; if they do, it may be for business since Samsung phones or Hyundai cars are sold everywhere. I use the term "mentality" since humans are animals deeply affected by environments – poor people have more reasons to be where they are than the wealthy. **We become poorer after expending on tourism.** I have watched many Americans going bankrupt after spending up life-savings in Thailand.

There is a travel writer named Park. He is the same age as I am, but the first country he visited was Mexico in 1994. He visited many countries in South America and wrote the first series[38] of books about it. Then, he visited

---

[38] Three volumes.

China and wrote his second series. What does he do now? He lives in a small village in Thailand without having savings or family. He has never married, and I can see that he worries about money all the time, according to his blog. Typically, these Koreans never get a job in Southeast Asia – they make some dough in Korea and stay as long as they can in those poor countries. If he visited the USA as the first foreign country and then Europe 30 years ago, would his life be different now? Possibly since Koreans in America are generally wealthier than those in Korea. The same goes for Americans: Americans in Switzerland may be wealthier than those in Cambodia.

In a sense, I am blessed that I happened to start my international travels with wealthy countries in 1997: USA, Denmark, Finland, Netherland and Japan. I did not realize this then, but these destinations were all for my studies or businesses. **I am glad not because I want to be rich, but because I might have avoided a chance to get poorer.** These experiences 30 years ago still affect me. Maybe poor people visit impecunious countries, to begin with. Or vice versa – **we become poor after visiting penurious countries repeatedly.**

For my international travels, I visited the USA for study in 1997; Denmark and Finland for business in 1998; the Netherlands and Japan were for layovers; Canada for tourism (mostly Toronto while I stayed in

Buffalo, NY for 5 years). I have lived in South Korea for 26 years and the USA for 24 years after that by 2023. Living in a country for decades is also a kind of travel since life is a journey, right?

* * *

The first time I went to Europe was in 1998. That was pretty much the first international trip. I went to RIT in Rochester, NY in 1997, which was purely for study. I still lived in Korea then and my father had owned a fur import business for more than 25 years. His company used to import mink from Denmark and fox furs from Finland. He was eager to find someone to inherit his business, so asked me and one of his employees to go on the business trip together. It was the right timing before I graduated from a college in South Korea.

Quite frankly, my father had an unpleasant hot temper and I had never gotten along with him for life – he had always been ready to be angry for anything. Often, there was no visible reason for his anger and I believe he should have controlled it even if there was a reason. He had done whatever he wanted to his family only because he made money and I was too young to live on my own. He was good at making money, though: **I don't think we should expect perfection from anyone.** The only problem was he had kept approaching me to ask to take over his business years after years even until I became 48.

Fur business has been dying in Korea. Did your mom wear a fur coat today? Does she have one at home? Probably not. The business has been dead everywhere in the world for decades now. In general, clothing productions move from wealthy countries to low income countries; for example, Vietnam makes T-shirts rather than Singapore. Then, the fur business has had another critical disadvantage: **Global warming.** Even the super-rich will not wear it unless the weather is *extremely* cold. Have you ever tried on a fur coat before? It had been invented for extremely cold weather, not for mildly cold ones.

In a sense, I am glad that he had a fur business, not a smartphone one. If I wanted to work with him, I would have done that already, regardless of a business type. It was a good excuse not to work with him: Fur had been a decaying business. Honestly, I am glad he did not have an IT business since I might not have a good excuse to stay away from him. I feel sorry for all those young people having unpleasant fathers: **I am glad that my father did not have a visionary business to leave**.

It is an undoubtable blessing that he made money, gave some to his two sons and gave me a chance to take a look around Northern Europe once in 1998: Denmark, Netherland and Finland. I was young and thought that I would be visiting Europe every now and then. But it was the only time and I am not sure when I can get out of

Illinois again. Once we are settled with our own family and busy with jobs or investments, I learned that it's nearly impossible to move around as before – we have to try hard even to get out of our houses with a child.

* * *

My father, one of his employees and I used KLM airline to Denmark in 1998. I liked the employee, Young-hu, from my father's company. He was two years older than me, had a gentle character and was kind to me probably because I was a son of his boss. I never had a problem with him for two weeks even though I had been with him all along from airplane to hotel rooms. But I had a hard time with my father if I had a chance to see him even for a second. I do not know what's wrong with this man since he had a business seat in the plane far from us and stayed in a separate hotel room as well. I felt like he existed to make others painful. Maybe that is what all the fur business is about - maybe that is what humans do to other animals.

I remember the Kimpo national airport in Korea was like a flea market in America then. Korea built a totally new airport in 2001 and it is the world's best even now. But it was still a poorer country back then. We were in a duty free shop and the retail glass counters were just like the ones we can see in flea markets - nothing fancy. These duty free girls tried to sell something like Ginsengs and said something in Japanese and my father answered,

"I am not Japanese." Japan was outstandingly richer then. I think it took about 15 hours to get to Copenhagen, Denmark. The customs officer said, "Good Evening" in perfect English. My father's sales agent (Jewish American) came to pick us up: I heard father bought a lot from him every year, who was nice, tall and fat. I met a lot of Jewish riches in the fur trading center buildings and learned that we do not have to be unnecessarily aggressive to get wealthy. As a middle aged man, **I suspect having a hot temper actually makes us lose money.**

It was pleasantly warm in Copenhagen although it was January, 1998. I would say it was like mild south Busan weather in Korea. I spent most of the day in the huge warehouse handling fur stocks. The place gave us hotel quality nice meals for free. Basically, hundreds of buyers came from all over the world and millions of dollars of purchases were made within a couple of weeks. There were a lot of auctions for fur packages from morning till evening. Young-hu and I helped my father to get all the stock samples to check and move them back to their original places.

I felt sorry for all those animals since probably about 200,000 minks are massacred every year and their skins were removed and dried there – it's more waste than people assume since no one eats mink meat. These animals were murdered purely for fur – I think humans are too selfish. Although this was not the primary reason why I don't work with my father, I am glad that I have not been part of this agony. I personally hope people keep wearing regular coats like me other than furs. Still, I cannot blame my father since I have lived fine thanks to his money. **He had done what he had to do to get out of hunger;** it is a luxury to talk about animal rights for the Korean war generation. There were about twenty Korean big buyers in the wholesaler until 1998. The number had been smaller and virtually my father was only Korean when I saw him the last in Toronto, Canada in 2005 – Chinese have become dominant, instead.

* * *

Luckily, I was free in the evening during the Denmark and Finland trip in 1998; my father hung out with other businessmen and Yong-hu usually stayed in the room. I had a chance to check around freely by myself. The first thing I noticed was people sleep extremely early in Denmark. Basically, **the entire city of Copenhagen was shut down at 6:00 PM every day**. I could deduce that Scandinavians are morning people – even most restaurants were closed, so I truly wondered where people eat their dinners. Only some Chinese restaurants and strip bars were still open. Soon, I learned that Denmark is an erotically open country, too.

While I walked around in the dark pointlessly, I found a place which looked like an adult movie theater on the street. I remember it did have a smaller movie screen and Danishs gathered watching adult movies. The general atmosphere was safe and friendly, though. It was definitely not like an American skid row. What was unique was the drinking bar, which was serving mostly beer in the theater. The bartender lady was totally naked. It was a bit old lady when I was there for the first time. But there were young girls when I went there two more times. In particular, the third girl raised her leg and put her foot on the bar, whenever a customer ordered a drink; she tried to expose herself more that way.

Also I found a similar Asian place in Denmark; these were the only places open, anyway. When I entered, I saw a small Asian lady behind a bar, who exposed her breasts totally; I saw that she served drinks and spoke with a Danish man. Then, another tall pretty girl came, so I had a chance to talk with her. She said she is originally from Malaysia and it is 800 Krone to spend some time with her[39], which was like $112 USD in 1998. She lifted her skirt and showed her butt, but I could not do anything. Actually, I had to leave the country for good after our business. I just had a friendly talk with her for a while. When I think about it, it is surprising that Malaysians go all the way up there to make money. I visited similar places in Finland, too. Although I didn't try anything costing money, all these are unique memories from the European trip that winter.

* * *

---

[39] It must be 2,000 Krone IN 2023, which is $250 USD.

Summary

1. It's not a good idea to start visiting poor countries for indulgence early in our lives.
2. While we don't have to work hard, we do not have to look downward and feel better comparing ourselves with impoverished people.
3. I don't think we should immigrate to poorer countries than our home states – decisions not based on common sense must bring misery.

Author's Note

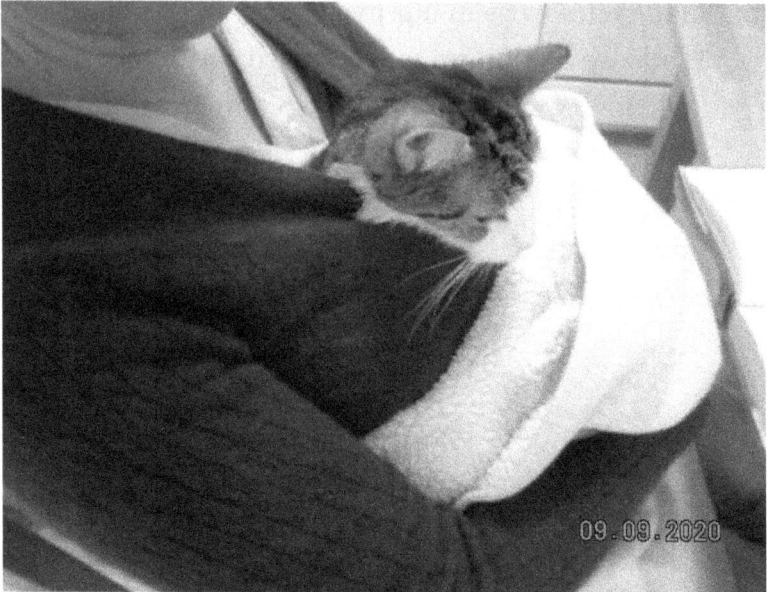

Congratulations: I truly appreciate you finishing my book until the end. The cat in the photo is Yang (Oscar) who I mentioned many times in Chapter 21 of *UnBrokable* III; it was taken only a few days before he passed away. We had so many memories, but he couldn't get over the blood cancer in the end.

I was born and raised in Korea and immigrated to America in my 20s; that was 24 years ago since it's 2023 now. In the beginning, I failed getting accepted to prestigious Ivy league schools although SUNYat Buffalo is a great school. Then I graduated from college with a 2.5 GPA by 2005, so I couldn't get into any graduate school as well. Then I started my own business, but it wasn't very successful for 8 years. Subsequently, my career at the nursing home also didn't work out as I planned even though I won two certificates during the 7 years; now I try to be a writer at the age of 49.

If you believe this book can be helpful to others and have a minute to spare, **I would truly appreciate a review or rating;** your help in spreading the word is greatly appreciated. Believe it or not, *I do read all the reviews and use them to improve my writings.* Reviews from readers like you make a huge difference; please let me know what you think. I sincerely wish my best luck to you!

Acknowledgment

I thank my wife Tsina who has stayed in the living room for the last 10 years. She says it's OK, but it must have been uncomfortable for her.

I also appreciate Amazon who has offered all the platforms to write without charge. I wouldn't have even been a writer if self-publishing was not invented. I thank Google for supporting the writing platform Doc.

Thank you for reading my books.

www.ingramcontent.com/pod-product-compliance
Lightning Source LLC
Chambersburg PA
CBHW022041190326
41520CB00008B/669